LEARN M

CW01376624

Toddler to Teen - Discover Practical Boundaries for Modern Parenting

Christina Lovemore

ABOUT THIS BOOK

I wanted to write a parenting book that was both entertaining and educational at the same time. A real-life look at how coping with a growing family can be challenging but fulfilling and rewarding too. This book covers all sorts of situations surrounding life with three children, all at different ages and stages of development. It is about how growing with your children and having insight into what makes them who they are is so important. My three children taught me never to categorise them under the same label. They are all different and the only common ground they have is their family ties.

Taking a deep dive into goals and family values may seem too business-like for many parents. However, with these principles in place, positive discipline and raising well-adjusted children takes on a new perspective.

Parenting, like Dorothy's journey through Oz, can be scary at times. Put on your ruby slippers, and with your heart in the right place, a brain to think through tough times and the courage of a lion, you can follow the yellow brick road. The positive parenting road to a magical place, a place called home.

How to Get the Best Out of This Book

Learn more Lovemore - Toddler to Teen is a unique parenting book. Through the pages of this book you can follow real life experiences of the Lovemore family and their parenting style.

Read through over 40 different themes that assist with parenting. Christina gives insights into parenting from the day your child arrives home as an infant, becomes a toddler, and finally enters the teen stage of becoming a young adult.

Here's how you can benefit from this book.

• Read a real story of a family and their different children at different ages and stages of growth.

• Have insight into school life through Christina Lovemore's teaching and counselling experiences.

• Look through the glossary of themes in the book and read over any that are of particular interest or concern. This is the perfect way to get familiar with specific themes like aggression at school, early starts to sex education or the effect of technology on children of all ages. These are just a few of the themes explored in this book.

- Link up with the Learn more Lovemore Parenting group and ask other questions you may have as a parent.

This book brings real stories and real experiences to the reader. It is just the beginning of a parenting journey with help and support on every page.

I would like to take the time to THANK YOU for purchasing this book. As an author, it means a lot to me! For this reason, I would like to send you a copy of **'The Ultimate Parenting Guide'** as an appreciation and gratitude. Click the link below for your **FREE COPY!**

THE ULTIMATE PARENTING GUIDE

For Parents with paperback & Hardcover

www.lovemoreservices.com

CONTENTS

INTRODUCTION

Congratulations, Mr and Mrs Lovemore, you are parents! The day you hear those words is the day your life changes forever. It is real—your newborn baby has arrived and is placed in your arms for the first time. You look down at your bundle of joy with unconditional love, wonder, and amazement.

I remember seeing two big, round eyes looking up at me and feeling the tight grip of a tiny hand around my finger. I was looking at my new baby girl. I had this huge burst of pride mixed with so many other emotions. This blessing was the start of a remarkable parenting journey. My daughter held my hand, and I knew there would be lessons to learn and bridges to cross, but we would do it all together.

Becoming a parent is life-changing. I felt grateful that I had some knowledge of child development through my psychology studies, but does some academic learning provide all there is to know? I was sure that experience would play a larger part in understanding parenting. Oprah Winfrey said, on an episode of her talk show:

*'Biology is the least of what makes
someone a mother.'*

As I went through the various stages of parenting, this made more and more sense to me. We are part of nature's plans. We follow the pattern of life on a journey with each child. Biologically we give our children their genetic make-up, but the real work begins when we start to raise our children and share our lives with them. This mysterious journey that we undertake is filled with challenges and learning curves.

Sharing is caring, they say, and I started journaling my experiences and finding guidelines as I began to understand my role as a parent. One thing I noticed with children is, they are not 'one size fits all'! Each child, even in one family, is an individual. I was grateful for practical learning experiences as an educator. Studies in child psychology and hands-on counselling skill courses have helped my understanding of child development. However, there is no substitute for real experience in the school of life.

I have always loved writing. Stories for kiddies and articles for blogs or parenting reports just filled a genuinely enjoyable niche. It was a natural part of being an educator to help parents with their problems and discuss different parenting styles. Each parent and child has individual needs. Family dynamics are different, and yet they are similar in so many ways. Parenting is always a fascinating topic of discussion. A get-together with parents is usually filled with 'war stories' about family life. The good, the bad, and the ugly seem to sum up these happy and sometimes sad tales.

I realised that most parents want to know similar things about parenting. Some guidelines they grew up with are traditional ways of raising children, handed down from generation to generation. Some are new ideas as knowledge increases and parents have more access to articles and books on parenting. The subject of raising great kids never runs out of material, but specific discussion points crop up often.

Topics like communication. Well, how do you communicate with a stubborn two-year-old? Boundaries and discipline in our modern world of technology are very widely discussed subjects. What do you allow as a parent, and what is strictly out of bounds? How do you help your child with things like peer pressure, bullying at school, and making good friendships? School issues and character development fall into the melting pot. How about difficult children and children with learning problems? Parents have many challenges and issues to deal with as they nurture and develop their children. I wanted to find ways to help families with these issues. Writing became a natural way of sharing my knowledge and experience.

Travelling, adapting to a new country, and adding to the family, increased the level of parenting responsibilities for me. Growing your family adds to the challenges you face. You hope you will slip smoothly from one age into the next, but the children's characters change, and each phase is so different. I remember often wondering about my middle child. How could she be so different from the firstborn? Did I change the recipe? My middle child was utterly opposite to her sister in so many ways. Her approach to life was overruled by stubborn behaviour and defiance. Then I heard about middle child syndrome. Yes, it seemed genuine to say there is such a thing as a middle-child syndrome! Dealing with the opposition and still sounding fair is a challenge as you juggle the children's different personalities.

Character development and understanding how children feel through their emotional patterns is essential part of parenting. We often hear about nature versus nurture. This topic is always heavily debated. Which is more vital? Nature and the genetics of a child, or nurture, how the children are intimately raised. There are still two sides to every story. Nature does give out different attributes and strengths or weaknesses to each individual. Genetics is a fascinating topic! Star qualities handed down from parents and grandparents are visible in so many world-renowned characters. This is one side of the story. However, the way children are nurtured and nourished is of significant importance too. There are many examples of rising stars who emerge from deprived backgrounds and stories of privileged children who sadly lost their way and had to fight to get back in the race. Finding a parenting style that suits your family is an essential and exciting part of being a parent. This is the kick-off point in this book. Chapter one is all about positive, healthy parenting and how parenting styles can influence children's behaviour and their approach to life.

Every parent thrives on those proud moments when their child shines at home or school. Watching the little cross-country runner come round the corner into the final leg of the race, and seeing that it is your child, makes your heart soar. However, parenting is not all about winning a big event; it is also about the small victories only you share with your child. Finding a balance between a win or lose and standing together is so important.

I love singing songs of encouragement. Catchy tunes, with a cheerful chorus, can be so uplifting. Singing along in the car can be a magical time together. A favourite of mine is Paul McCartney's 'Frog Song'. He wrote the song to celebrate with Rupert Bear, and the chorus line goes like this:

'Win or lose,

Sink or swim,

One thing is certain

We'll never give in

Side by side,

Hand in hand

We all stand together.'

Children who know their parents stand with them just have that extra edge of confidence. Learning how to win or lose is an important life lesson.

How do our children learn these lessons? How do parents find the best solutions to difficulties they may face? The more I read about parenting, and the more experiences I had with my children, the more I realised I wanted to write a book. Not just any book on parenting, but a book sharing ideas, possible solutions, and information about being a mum and a dad.

This book invites you to join me for a series of chapters on parenting problems. I bring real-life stories based on my sixteen years of parenting and dedication to education while raising my own family. It is a subject I feel inspired to write about. I hope to share ideas and practical suggestions on this broad and fascinating topic through this book's chapters.

I hope you will join me on this parenting adventure through the medium of this book and my real-life experiences: the joys and sorrows, the pleasure and pain of parenting.

This is my masterclass!

Welcome, and let us stand together to raise extraordinary kids in our modern world.

CHAPTER ONE

THE MOST IMPORTANT PARENTING PRINCIPLES

The discharge forms had been filled in, the bouquets of flowers collected, and now was the defining moment. I was leaving the maternity ward to go out into the world with my newborn baby. My life was about to change forever! The exceedingly kind nurse pushed my baby out to the reception area in a hospital bassinet. Like an umbilical cord, we were still connected to the medical team. The car was waiting, and I eased my way into the back seat. Only then was my baby given gently to me. I could sense my husband rushing around in the background with bags and baggage, but I was focused on my baby. This was it, one small step out of the hospital and a giant leap into parenthood!

Although I had prepared myself for this event with maternity classes, baby books, magazines, parenting blogs, and every possible form of instruction available, this was still a genuine moment for me. A slight grunt from the bundle I was holding reminded me the baby was alive. She wriggled a bit and made another snuffle noise. Oh, please do not let her cry, I thought. We are not even out of the car park yet. Then my husband was in the driver's seat. I saw him grinning from ear to ear, and I smiled. Yes, this parenting thing was for the two of us. The car lurched forward, and off we drove with the safety of the hospital fading into the background.

I had a flashback moment to my childhood. A poem we all had to learn. It was a punishment meted out by my parents. Naughty children were sent to the bathroom for some time out and to learn a few lines of Rudyard Kipling's poem—I could only remember the first few lines, but they were reassuring at that moment:

> *'If you can keep your head when all about you*

> *Are losing theirs and blaming it on you,*

> *If you can trust yourself when all men doubt you,*

> *But make allowance for their doubting too.'*

Another look in the rear-view mirror confirmed my suspicions. My husband was as nervous as I was. He shot past the driveway to our home. For a second, I thought he had changed his mind and was taking us back to the hospital.

'Honey, there are no returns on this model,' I said with a chuckle.

It was a comic relief moment as he realised what he had done and drove around the block to get back to the house. Driving around the block was going to become one of our regular outings at a later stage. We were unaware of its significance at the time.

We were home! The nursery had been waiting for this day. The crisp little crib was sweet, with soft teddies and toys waiting for a playmate. It all looked so beautiful, and now there was a real baby to put in the crib. My husband parked the car and came bursting into the nursery. Instinctively I put my fingers on my lips to hush his deep voice. We were ready to tiptoe around like two little hush puppies. Then I shook my head, lay the baby in the crib, and smiled at my husband. Our baby was home, but we didn't have to turn into jelly. We could do this—together.

It was amazing! After a few days of adjusting to this new person in our home, we began to relax. There were visitors and eager grandparents to deal with. How interesting it was to see our parents turn all mushy and soppy with their first grandchild. Our daughter's paternal grandparents were outdoorsy, bush-loving kinds of rugged people. A handshake from this grandpa left you wondering if your knuckles were permanently crushed. The moment he faced the new baby, he just melted into a cooing softie. I could see his granddaughter had him wrapped around her little finger in seconds. My mum was a star, loving the new baby but looking out for me simultaneously. Now I was a mother too. Mum had recently remarried, and it was beautiful to see her happy and relaxed with Reggie, our stepdad. It would be interesting to hear the kind of parenting advice they would come up with.

I had entered a whole new world. There seemed to be babies, toddlers, and new mums around every corner. Conversations at family events and getting together with friends revolved around baby milestones. I used to avoid the 'mum's corner' at parties. Now I was drawn towards this group. I found myself eagerly listening to the snippets of information. Parenting just became more complex. There were so many different ways to be a parent. It made me think more about how I grew up. What was the norm for then? Did those tried-and-trusted parenting tips apply today? Finding out about parenting styles would be helpful, I decided.

I realised every parent wants the same end result for their child. When I was growing up, positive parenting meant positive children. A sort of input and output guide to reach the end goal of a positive parent/child relationship. The trouble was how to start and what environment was needed for this positive cycle? Who do you turn to in times like these? I thought my mum could be the right place to start.

The next time Mum came around, I asked her.

> '*So, Mum, who did you consult for parenting advice? Did you have a special paediatrician you looked up to?*'

My mother's reply came as a shock. Yes, it was a name I had heard of, but I never thought it was a name connected to parenting and raising healthy children.

> *'Doctor Spock,' replied Mum.*

I was horrified.

> *The Star Trek alien with big ears from an old TV show? No, it couldn't be Dr Spock. Did an alien raise me?*

My mum saw my horrified face, and she began to laugh. She explained that Dr Spock was a real doctor and had nothing to do with the TV show. Well, that was a relief! However, I did want to understand parenting styles and find a style that suited my family. It was time to investigate positive parenting.

Parenting styles, parenting blogs, books on parenting issues, and so many other resources are available. I set out to read through several publications to understand what this mantra of 'positive parenting' meant. Where to begin and what to implement. Psychologists have narrowed parenting styles down to four categories:

1. **Authoritarian/disciplinarian:** A strict authoritarian style, not very nurturing; involves corporal punishment with a 'do as I say' set of rules.

2. **Permissive/indulgent:** The opposite of the first style, warm and nurturing. Children are allowed input into their lifestyle.

3. **Uninvolved:** Lots of freedom, little involvement or guidance from parents.

4. **Authoritative:** Rules are clear, communication is important, a nurturing style.

Each of these styles has its own approach to parenting—a philosophy, but not one that most parents would want to follow too rigidly. As you read them, you find yourself thinking: too strict, too casual, or too distant. A bit like Goldilocks trying to find the perfect chair, there must be one that is 'just right!' Is there one that fits your family and children? That is what makes parenting such a challenge! There is never a hard and fast approach. You may have theories handed down from your parents, and you may even catch yourself saying things to your children that your parents told you.

I clearly remember these sayings and the thoughts I had at the time:

'Money doesn't grow on trees.'

Always popular when you need something for school or an outing.

'I wasn't born yesterday!'

In your rebellious teenage mind, you were thinking, *Not yesterday but pretty close to a time before the wheel!*

'Just wait till your father gets home!'

Fortunately for us, our dad came home late. The incident was over, and our mum usually forgot.

'Stop crying, or I'll give you something to cry about.'

This was a popular one if we were whining or carrying on about something. It usually worked, and then we were quiet

'When I was your age....'

After which would follow a list of old-fashioned ways of going to school or earning pocket money, favourites were riding in a donkey cart and weeding the lawn. My father-in-law had many things he had to do to survive his childhood, and he delighted in sharing them with us.

Funny little quips remind us of past parenting styles. We do remember some of the ways our parents raised us because it is part of our history. We do not have to implement their style. There may be some positives handed down the parenting line, but generally speaking, times have changed so incredibly. Technology has changed our generation, and standards of education have progressed dramatically. Parenting styles must vary too. How was I going to do it better, smarter, and more effectively?

This quote from Frederick Douglas, an African-American abolitionist and writer, sticks in my mind as a good leveller. It made me think about the importance of solid parenting.

He said:

> *'It is easier to build strong children than to repair broken men.'*

Building children up! That must be the way to go. They will be growing so fast, and our parenting styles will have to grow with them. You never stop being a parent! Each stage of your child's life is going to be different. That's inevitable, but perhaps some basic principles are out there to raise different children in different circumstances. Fundamental principles to apply that will always make a difference and set a standard for the family.

I was a little concerned about some of the parenting situations we might find ourselves in as our children grew up. Naturally, our parents' parenting would have an effect. The way we grew up would influence how we parent our children. We had different backgrounds, and our parents were quite different in their outlook. My husband grew up on a farm. The children had the freedom of the farm but went to boarding school from a young age. Discipline was very relaxed in my husband's family. However, I do remember him saying that my father-in-law was supposed to have had a temper and shouted at the boys, my husband and his three brothers.

My father spent a great deal of time away from home. Sadly, he could not control his addiction to alcohol, and Mum was left alone to raise us independently. It was up to me to become the surrogate mother figure as Mum was working hard for us. These were not ideal circumstances, but I soon became capable of running the home. Mum worked hard so that my brother and I could get a good education.

Putting all these different parenting experiences into a melting pot meant our initial parenting styles would need some discussion. My background was with a single mum out at work most of the time, and my husband's outdoor life was combined with boarding school. We both had quite different growing-up experiences. My parenting aim was for a well-rounded child raised with love and respect. I hoped we could agree on that.

It was going to be essential to discuss significant discipline issues as parents and partners in raising our daughter. We would need to agree before we impose any disciplinary action, and sometimes there may be conflict about our choices. When I had compiled my tick list of parenting skills, I would share it with my dear hubby so that we could be a team. We would need to remember the following:

- NO ARGUING IN FRONT OF THE CHILDREN ON MATTERS OF DISCIPLINE.

- AGREE ON A PLAN OF ACTION AND CONSEQUENCES OF MISBEHAVIOUR.

- DECIDE ON A STYLE OF PARENTING AND FUNDAMENTAL PRINCIPLES.

- SUPPORT EACH OTHER IN FRONT OF THE CHILDREN.

- BE FLEXIBLE AND ACKNOWLEDGE THAT SOMETIMES EVERYONE MAKES MISTAKES.

These essential elements of good parenting, combined with the fundamentals, would make the right support formula for our parenting skills. I needed a list, a tick list that would enable me to try to check parenting skills. I do like a tick list! Finding some basic ideas and itemising them was my idea of a good strategy.

I identified ten principle points to apply to parenting at any stage of development. That is what makes this list so helpful and pertinent. It is a cornerstone for parenting.

As I read through these points, I thought of my family circumstances. I realised they could apply to the neonatal stage as well as the toddler and early-childhood phase. They would be helpful as children grew older. I felt they would match my family as I added more children to the team. These principles spoke of laying an excellent foundation for parenting and a family lifestyle. Ready for different ages and stages, I would go through on my parenting journey. This was my idea of a good solid foundation, and it could be a tick list too.

TEN FUNDAMENTAL PRINCIPLES OF GOOD PARENTING

1. Actions often speak louder than words.

2. Love conquers all. Parents cannot be too loving.

3. Get down and dirty. Be involved at every stage.

4. Set rules and guidelines that everyone knows.

5. Be ready to be adaptable. Adjust according to your child's stage in life.

6. Help your child to become responsible and independent.

7. Try not to be erratic. Consistent behaviour makes children feel secure.

8. Take time to explain the rules and the decisions you make.

9. Harsh discipline can have a negative effect. Try to be firm but fair.

10. Earn respect as a parent by treating your child with respect.

Now I wondered if all ten of these fundamentals could apply to every parenting situation and different lifestyles. I decided to 'unpack' each idea and give them a tick if they did. Would the list get 10/10 and gold stars? A little bit of the teacher came out in me as I looked at the list with an objective eye. As parents, we need to be objective while remembering we are here as guardians and carers to our children. We are a support to launch them into the real world. Our job as parents is to give our children wings so they can eventually fly on their own.

- **Actions speak louder than words**: Without a doubt, they do, especially to the toddler or infant still coming to grips with language skills. Every act of my parenting must speak of my values and my concern for my child. I remembered how thoughtful my mum had always been when I was growing up. It was not with the big things, but with little things. During exam time, she would pack me a little snack with a note in my lunch box just to say she was thinking of me and hoping the exam questions would be just the ones I wanted. Sometimes the letter would say 'surprise when you get home.' When I arrived, the smell of freshly baked muffins would waft out of the kitchen. It made me feel loved while the exams were on. I wanted to remember that often it is the little things that mean the most.

- **Love conquers all**: There is no doubt that everyone grows up better with lots of love. Love is not the smothery kind of love; it is so much more. Acts of service and spending quality time with my child will be expressions of love too. I tried to keep a loving eye on Kerry all the time while she was a toddler. One day I heard an almighty yell coming from the storeroom. I rushed to the door to find Kerry had opened her daddy's toolbox and taken out the hammer. She had dropped it on her toe! There was a terrified look in her eyes because she knew she was not allowed to play with her daddy's tools.

'Mummy cross?' she asked, with tears welling up in her eyes.

It was a 'love conquers all' moment. I gave her a big hug and explained I should be cross, but I was also sad for her sore toe. We laughed together and put the toolbox away. I think Kerry had learned her lesson, and a big hug was what was really needed at that time.

- **Get down and dirty:** Yes, I may have to get into 'child's pose' for this one. Being involved in my child's everyday life will mean some dirty work, but I am sure my children will appreciate my involvement at each age. I found my children loved making things together. Papier mâché playdough and building sandcastles were all messy fun. It was during these playtimes that I could talk to my children and hear all sorts of exciting things about how they felt at school and home.

- **Setting out rules and guidelines:** Letting children know what is allowed and where to draw the line is essential. I read in more than one publication that setting out the policies is a vital aspect of parenting. Starting early, from the moment my child could understand about rules, would benefit everyone. Have you ever played a game with someone who does not stick to the rules? It can be very frustrating and confusing. Having a game plan that keeps pace with the family's growing needs is an integral part of regulations and guidelines. Setting family goals is a way of keeping the best rules in mind aiming for positive parenting.

- **Being ready to be adaptable:** This is such a necessary point of view. It is a parenting requirement as children do not stay the same. Every day is different, and every stage offers its own set of highs and lows. The baby phase goes by in a flash.

Beware of wishing for the next stage. Suddenly your baby is grown up, and you have missed some of those precious milestones. Being adaptable has to get a star rating. It is a must from toddler to teen; being flexible is very important.

Those early crawling days were some of the most challenging. I remember having to adapt to the fact that at this stage, EVERYTHING goes straight into the baby's mouth. I had to have eyes in the back and top of my head. Even the toys we bought from the shops were a challenge. I wondered how to avoid toys that could choke. Then by chance, I read about this excellent guide. The way to measure if a toy is a choking hazard or not is to see if the toy will fit through a toilet roll tube. If it fits through, then it has the potential to choke the baby. I hastily took out all Kerry's toys and did the tube test with them. Any toy or block or shape that would fit through that toilet roll was removed from the toy basket.

I felt proud of myself that day for adapting to Kerry's needs and being certain her toys were safe too. It was a small act of awareness that set me up to be aware of changes and adaptations as my child grew and developed.

- **Aim for an independent and responsible child:** Yes, a definite goal to have in mind. This aspect of parenting comes to the fore with potty training, which is probably the first time your toddler is ready to show some independence and responsibility. Cultivate these attributes and see how to carry them over into other activities. A parent should not be overprotective and should enable a child to take responsibility for their actions. Independence is also essential as children today are faced with a bigger world and more decisions of their own to make.

- **Consistent behaviour is a crucial factor:** Definitely, one of the challenges of parenting in any family is being consistent. Children find it difficult to settle into a tranquil routine when a parent is responding differently. Yes, we all have meltdowns and moments of frustration, but I knew I would try to keep them in check. I would need to find my own space to have my little rant and rave. Good advice suggested that if I did have an emotional outburst, I would try to reassure my child and explain what triggered the reaction.

- **Explain rules and decisions:** It is not always easy to bring logic into the world of a two-year-old, but as children grow older, they do learn to understand consequences. Following rules make more sense if they are logical and understood. We were told as children, 'It is what it is!' Well, that did not help much and led to rebellion and a feeling of, well, it was just what it was. I didn't want my kiddos growing up feeling regimented and facing confusion over 'what is.'

- **Discipline:** 'Spare the rod and spoil the child.' That's what I remember from my parents and grandparents. Severe punishment is very old-fashioned. There has to be a better way to raise good citizens. In biblical times, where this piece of parenting advice originated, I found an interesting link to shepherding. The rod was not there to beat the sheep. The rod was for guiding and protecting. That stuck in my mind, and I decided that I would not spare the rod based on a goal of guidance. The analogy of a rod would be a reminder of gently caring for my flock. The rod would stem from the principles I was going to use for parenting basics.

- **Earn respect:** I definitely wanted a star for this point. I came across this quote by Lawrence Goldstone, an American writer, who said,

'You can demand courtesy, but you have to earn respect.'

If I was going to earn respect, I knew it would be an ongoing principle to put in place. The concerns of a toddler would be different from a teen!

Wow, would I get 10/10 and stars for my parenting principles? Probably not, because this was going to be a work in progress. Teaching and learning through the pupils I had taught was a good starting point, but parenting was another ball game. 'The real deal,' as they say. While trying not to be too philosophical, a song popped into my head. It was one of my mum's favourites. 'Getting to Know You' from *The King and I*. A real 'back in the day' movie, but Mum used to sing it often as we grew up.

'Getting to know you,' followed by
'Aaaah' as the children joined in.

'Getting to know all about you,' another
'Aaaah', and we used to join in the
chorus.

'Getting to like you,

Getting to hope you like me.

Getting to know you,

Putting it my way,

But nicely,

You are precisely,

My cup of tea....'

Aaaah, I loved that song and the memories it brought of Mum singing while pottering around the kitchen.

A loud cry from the nursery brought me back to reality. I was getting to know all about my new baby. Yes, I thought, as I dressed her in a pretty pink baby-grow, she is precisely my cup of tea.

We had named our first baby Kerry, Kerry Ann. A hint of Irish for my family roots and a name that resonated with her dark hair, brown eyes, and hopefully a touch of the Irish good luck and happiness.

If I was going to earn respect, I knew it would be an ongoing principle to put in place. The concerns of a toddler would be different from a teen!

CHAPTER TWO

PRACTICE PERCEIVING THE WORLD FROM YOUR CHILD'S PERSPECTIVE

The first time my baby smiled at me, not one of the wobbly, windy smiles, but a genuine grin, was the first time I began to feel a connection. I wondered what my baby saw. Did she see my tired eyes after being up all night attending to her needs, or my face calm and content, gazing down at her sweet, little rosebud lips?

Everything had been a roller coaster experience as I graduated from the maternity ward to reach home with a new baby. *What does my baby see in her small world?* I wondered as I looked around at toys and mobiles, and other colourful objects. Baby's vision is a bit of a blur, and parents need to get up close and personal to be in the line of focus. A baby's world is a very small one at this stage. I discovered that if I wanted to be in her line of vision, I would need to remember that a baby can't focus on fast-moving objects. I looked carefully at my little one gazing up at me, and I realised she would not see colour for a while. I assured myself that it was a good thing and ceased to worry about make-up!

My baby was growing and developing at an astonishing rate. I wondered what it was like in her world. At first, a world of breastfeeding and nurturing in every way, then trying to crane her neck to see new things. Kerry's world must have become a whole lot more exciting when some solid foods were added. I had to laugh when she ate the first baby spoon of porridge. What a face. Then came the aeroplane spoons that her dad insisted on using to get the endless bowls of pumpkin into her pursed lips. She had definite ideas about food.

I read that when my baby reaches the one-year milestone, she can see just like me! She would have proper 20/20 vision with Technicolor and 3D and all! There were some developmental steps to get there, from fuzzy pictures to recognising moving objects and seeing colour, shape, and size. Developments in vision would open up Kerry's world, although it was still a small world. How lucky was I, as her parent, to have the fantastic opportunity to help my child grow into that world?

Disney fans out there will recognise the kiddie's song 'It's A Small World (After All)'. Did you know that this is the single most widely performed song on the planet? It was composed for the 'It's a Small World' ride at the Disney theme parks. This song has been translated, transcribed, and used in all sorts of different situations. It has no copyright and pops up all over the place. You might catch yourself humming it, and once you know the melody and the simple lyrics, your brain will be hopelessly tuned in.

'There is just one moon

And one golden sun.

And a smile means

Friendship to everyone!'

It is catchy and a cute reminder that a baby's world is small—after all.

Although Walt Disney captures the small world essence so creatively in his songs and movies, a child's world is full of so much more. Magical wonders surround each stage of development. As parents, we have a responsibility to help our children experience the wonders of their world. It is a bit like a network of rings starting from the inner circle of birth and then adding on rings as the baby grows and develops through different phases.

Shakespeare had this summed up in his rendering of 'All the world's a stage.'

The men and women are merely players, making their exits and entrances.

'At first, the infant, mewling and puking
in the nurse's arms;

And then the whining schoolboy, with
his satchel

And shining morning face, creeping like
a snail

Unwillingly to school....'

I didn't want to go further than that. I did want to make the first
stage of Kerry's entrance into the world something unique. I
tried to help Kerry use all her senses to enjoy the world she was
living in. Mother and baby, I discovered, had plenty of adjusting
to do to their new world. As I sat feeding my baby, I wondered
how much of my psychology background would help me raise
this incredible new being.

Psychology has taught me many things about child development.
The whole debate of nature and nurture is always an exciting
topic. Cultural, social, and socio-economic factors influence
child development. Genetics plays its part, and I wondered what
my child would inherit from her parents and grandparents. There
seemed to be a balance of sport and artistic talent in the family. It
would be an exciting tussle to see which genetics were more
dominant and how much cultural influences would play their
part.

Naturally, the immediate family would have the most influence
on Kerry as she watched her parents interact. She would be part
of our traditions, cultural interests, and activities we deemed
essential. She had rough and tumble times ahead with two
healthy little boy cousins. My husband came from a big family,
and gatherings with his family were noisy outdoor affairs. My

mum was the other grandparent, with a smaller but still influential family side.

Actual influences on a child's life begin right from the early days of pregnancy. I had been rather scathing of playing classical music to the unborn child, but when I discovered the baby could hear in the uterus, I had a new respect for the mother's influence on the growing infant.

One of the responsibilities I took seriously was the intrauterine experience my baby had. I knew it was essential to make sure the nine months the baby spent in my uterus were the real beginnings of her development. I learned some interesting things about how my baby was growing even before she was born!

WWW—the Wonderful World of the Womb. Imagine if we could tune in and have conversations with our newborns before they entered the world.

Fetal movement is most exciting as the first signs of life are apparent. A quickening or full-blown kick are the signs of life 'mums-to-be' are looking for. Sharing the first kicks is a fascinating time, and when your partner gets to feel them too, he begins to feel a part of this whole process. Whether you have a ballet dancer or a soccer player will not matter in the least.

When the due date arrives, the baby will be entering a whole new world. According to psychologists and child developers, this next phase after the intrauterine experience is the infant stage. My love of journaling would be sure to come into play here, and with baby journals in hand and so much to describe in those early days, I was ready to record all the stages of development.

I thought I would start by putting the child's world into perspective and making some mental notes of how each stage should be. There are five key phases in terms of development, and here I was at phase number one. The bottom of the ladder and ready to climb upward following each stage of my child's development. Childhood can be grouped into five stages according to child developmental milestones.

I love this piece of wisdom from Dr Seuss, author of so many delightful children's books. He just had such a brilliant way with words:

'A person's a person no matter how small.'

I would remember that as I worked my way through the different childhood stages with my daughter. She looked tiny right now, but Dr Seuss was right; she was just a small person. What pearls of wisdom could I find from my psychology lectures? Perhaps there would be coping skills I could attach to each of these phases? Now that would be a help in the future.

Understanding the different developmental stages is a critical factor in parenting, and I thought psychology would help. My husband thought differently, but he was supportive of my parenting books and references to what I had learned at university.

These stages are best described as growth milestones. Everyone needs some sort of coping mechanism as they take on this parenting journey.

These five stages are listed as Infant, Toddler, Pre-school, Primary or formal school, and becoming an Adolescent.

STAGE ONE: INFANT

Parents are very hands-on at this stage. Infants can do very little for themselves. They depend on their parents for nurture and warmth, for protection and social interaction. The first year of a child's life is the infant stage. I looked at my baby and couldn't believe that she would learn to sit, crawl, and stand in one year. She would get teeth and start making different sounds. The first year meant learning to laugh and clap hands to interact with people.

The fantastic game of peek-a-boo is such a family favourite. I discovered this little game is significant in child development. It helps with anticipation of what comes next and the idea that something can disappear yet still be there as it comes back into view. This is called object permanence. Imagine a crucial skill, and it's all learned through a game called peek-a-boo. The joyous laughter that follows the game is the bonus for the happy parent.

Have you ever wondered about the origins of this childish game? I discovered it comes from a French game called Pique-a-beau. It was not really a game. A young French girl would show displeasure towards her boyfriend, or beau, by covering her face, pretending to hide from him.

Coping skills

What would be the best coping skill for parents at this stage?

Being attuned: Learning the technique of being adjusted is a beneficial skill. Mothers are naturally attuned to their baby's cries and coughs and sneezes, but being attuned is more than just being able to 'tune in' to another person or sound. It is an emotional connectedness. It is all about building relationships through verbal and non-verbal cues. A smile, some laughter, soft sounds of encouragement all develop that emotional connection. Being attuned to your infant helps develop their brain into making sense of their early emotions. Have you wondered why people go all gooey over a baby? Their faces get soft and mushy, and they make cooing noises. It is all part of being attuned.

STAGE TWO: TODDLERS

The terrible twos! The age of exploration and trying to find their way in this world. It is a big world out there, and now a toddler gets to move around and explore! Toddlers are busy little people. My daughter never sat still for a moment. I remember my mum telling me that when Kerry started to toddle, we would have to raise our living standards. I was not quite sure what she meant; it was a struggle keeping things together on a day-to-day basis. One income at the moment and a strict budget. How could I possibly raise our standard of living? Mum had a twinkle in her eyes as she began to pick up the coffee table books and move the glass bowl to a higher place in the lounge.

'That is raising the standard of living. It would be best if you put precious ornaments and books at a higher level for a while,' said Mum.

I knew that to be good advice given in a kindly way. There was no point in arguing with a two-year-old. Having unnecessary temptations in the way just made things worse. Coping with this young explorer and how quickly she could move from place to place required patience.

Coping skills

What would be the best toddler coping skill? I looked through some of the little notes I had jotted down in my journal and read things like:

- Knocked over the table
- Spread mud across the floor
- Pulled all the toilet paper off the roll
- Dug the new geranium out of the pot plant holder

Yes, I knew just the coping skill for the toddler stage—patience. Lots and lots of patience.

Patience: Is patience a skill? I remember reading patience is a virtue, but could patience be something you could learn. Perhaps knowing how patience helps in challenging situations would make the need for patience seem more relevant and worth trying to acquire.

Top of the list of patience tools is deep breathing and trying to relax. That is a challenge with a highly active toddler running around. However, I read that patience puts you in control of a situation, and that is how you score more advantages over your robust toddler. It has been said that a toddler can do more in one unsupervised minute than most people do in a day! I tried to keep up with my toddler and factor in that I had limitations. Realistically, a mum with a toddler cannot take on too much. I had to recognise my limits and not take on too much in one day.

Added to the relax and deep breathing advice, I found these three useful tips:

1. Stop doing things that are not important at the time.

2. Take note of the things that make you feel impatient.

3. Practice waiting for a bit. A count of ten, or three if there is not that much time, may just diffuse your impatient response.

There is a Greek proverb that says, 'One minute of patience, ten years of peace.' I am sure one minute of patience and ten minutes of peace would sound useful to toddlers' parents!

STAGE THREE: PRE-SCHOOL

This was an incredible stage to reach. My toddler was becoming more humanised. We were ready for school. Well, her mum was, and my little girl seemed eager to step out into the world of learning. I discovered several different names for this beginning phase of education: pre-primary, nursery school, or playschool. Play and school were confusing elements for parents because so many eager mums and dads could not put the idea of play and school together. Luckily, my training in pre-school education and early childhood learning helped with understanding these phenomena of playing and learning at the same time.

'When we make play the foundation of learning, we teach the whole child.' A quote from Vince Gowmon, who wrote a great book on nurturing the creative spirit in children.

Coping skills

What is the best way to get the most out of this stage? Probably making time to play and be playful as you watch your preschooler get the foundation they need for learning.

Playfulness: Would you find it difficult to be playful and enter the world of imagination and frivolity with your child? It may be for some parents who are eager to get their child reading or saying their ABC's and having a structured education. This is the stage of learning through play. We had such great times together with imaginary tea parties and playing 'baker' by cooking and decorating biscuits in the kitchen.

Making imaginary tents and houses under the dining room table was another favourite time together. Somewhat backbreaking, but I could see my daughter loved it when her daddy got down on his knees and crawled into the tiny house or tent she had made.

A dressing-up box was one of the best investments for fantasy play. I raided my mum's collection of old hats and bags. Then I found some old shoes, and my daughter was in her element, dressing up and pretending to be all sorts of imaginary characters. A basket of puppets was added to the fantasy corner in the playroom. We had many lovely puppet shows. Fostering language development and a love of stories is a great benefit of having puppets to play with. This age is so ready to enjoy storybook characters and acting out all their favourite stories.

The best time of the day was always going to be bedtime. Not only because it was the end of a busy day, but because sleep time meant story time. Reading stories and encouraging a love of books has to be the most precious learning tool any parent can give to their child. Turning pages and hearing well-loved fairy tales, as well as laughing over funny picture books and nursery tales, was just the most rewarding experience.

While looking back on childhood memories, this phase was a precious time with early learning experiences. It was a time to get ready for the next step forward in my child's world. The more we could play and learn, the better. I added some ballet lessons for my daughter because I could not resist seeing her in a tutu, and she loved dancing. We had dancing lessons just for fun. It is essential to have fun at this early development stage and not have a heavily organised itinerary. Ballet classes were not for any pressurised intentions of grandeur in the ballet world.

The moment any activity becomes a mission of dragging little ones to vast numbers of organised 'lessons', then the essence of play and learning is lost. This phase disappears all too soon, and suddenly it is time for formal school or 'big school' and a transition to the next stage in a child's world.

STAGE FOUR: FORMAL SCHOOL

What did this phase of my child's world look like? As a mum, trying to do all the right things, and a teacher too, this was a critical phase. My child was going to sail through school. I was so prepared with the right choice of school, the uniforms (all marked, of course), and the perfect stationery for the ideal little schoolgirl. Day one went according to plan, and then on day two, my child had a complete meltdown.

I was horrified. How did this happen? I thought I had school all under control. The trouble was, I had not tried to see this from my child's point of view. It was all about me and what I wanted from starting school. Indeed, I needed to go back to basics and the coping skill of being attuned. What was my daughter feeling, and what did it seem like from her perspective?

Once I realised her little world of pre-school had become a much bigger world of more children, more formality, and a very different routine, I was able to get down to her level. I had to understand how to help with this introduction to a big school. Looking at school through a child's eyes in first grade helps understand how and why there may be tears and trepidation initially.

Coping skills

I wondered what was going to get me to understand the formal school stage the best. Was it academic knowledge or sporting ability? Could it be an appreciation of music or the arts? There would be a great deal going on at a big school: friendships, peer pressure, academic pressure, and more. The balance came to mind. The formal school would be a balancing act.

Balancing: Parents with school-going children must find out how to balance so many different things. There are new schedules, early reading, and maths skills to learn. Then along comes homework! Balancing sports commitments, parent-teacher interviews, and probably another child at home is in the mix. Yes, this stage was a balancing act. I felt very heartbroken for the mums who had to go back to work and juggle all these activities and be part of their child's world at this stage.

Dr Seuss came to mind again with one of his catchy little verses, but one with the balancing concept:

'Step with care and great tact

And remember that Life's A Great Balancing Act.

Just never forget to be dexterous and deft.

And never mix up

Your right foot with your left.'

A touch of humour always gets me through a difficult situation, making the balancing act a little easier to handle. My daughter wanted to be part of everything once she got over the first emotional introduction to 'big school'. She enjoyed all the extra-murals and the dramatics of primary school too. I remember remonstrating with my mum about another school play costume. Kerry wanted to take part in everything! My mum reminded me of a little person she knew who had to have the best robin costume for her role in 'The Red Robin'.

Mum said she spent hours on feathered wings and all sorts of red leotard material. The robin costume was perfect. Then on the great day of the show, my mum found the other children had a single feather in their hair and brown tracksuits.

We had a good laugh about that, and it helped me remember the balancing act.

STAGE FIVE: ADOLESCENT

The child's world seems to disappear into a whirl of hormonal turbulence and emotional outbursts at the onset of puberty and adolescence. It almost felt as if I was back at the terrible twos. Adolescents are trying to find their place in the world, and parenting becomes incredibly challenging.

This was the development stage that drew on all my psychology training, including what is known as reverse psychology. The adolescent is a very reactive person. Mature one moment and immature the next. Emotional outbursts are common. The teenager needs help managing the challenges of growing up in a world surrounded by technology and peer pressure. This made the final stage of my child's world a very challenging but simultaneously exciting experience.

Coping skills

'All of the above' was what came to mind. I needed all the coping skills I had learned along the way. Raising my children to get to the teen years would help me view the world from an adolescent's perspective. I read a quote somewhere, an anonymous one, that said:

'Raising teenagers is like nailing Jell-O to a tree!' I did not want a relationship with my daughter to become a slippery mess.

Communication: Communication was what seemed to be the most crucial aspect of dealing with this adolescent phase. Mindful parents who ensure that children develop these communication lines from an early age was the next most vital part of understanding parenting solutions.

CHAPTER THREE

THEY MAY HEAR YOU, BUT ARE YOUR KIDS LISTENING...?

C ommunicating & talking to my child was a magical part of her development. I just loved how Kerry soaked up new words, and we started to share little conversations. It was incredible how many new comments were added to her vocabulary every day. Then I saw the movie 'Look Who's Talking. 'I was fascinated by the idea of being able to talk to your child from the moment they are born. In the movie, the baby called Mikey starts talking about life from a child's perspective as he makes a dramatic entrance into the world. Bruce Willis is Mikey's voice, and baby Mikey is very indignant about arriving into the world.

'Help! Put me back!' yells the newborn Mikey.

Mikey continues to make entertaining comments throughout the movie. He has such funny things to say about life through a baby's eyes. There were two sequels to the 'Look Who's Talking' movies. In 'Look Who's Talking Too', Mikey gets a baby sister and feels left out. Then in the third and final movie, 'Look Who's Talking Now', their pets join in the conversations. The family adopts a street dog and a pedigree poodle.

If we could communicate with our children from the moment they were born, we could gain insight into their world and what they were thinking. Speaking with Kerry was so rewarding. We developed a beautiful mother-daughter bond. When I discovered I was pregnant with my second child, I knew the household dynamics were going to change! Communication was going to be particularly important.

Kerry could talk, and as I waited for a new baby to arrive, I thought I would cast my eyes back on the child developmental stages and remind myself how babies learn words and language so they can talk. We were in for our own sequel, 'Look Who's Talking 2', with another sibling arriving.

How do children learn to talk?

Language is acquired. How do children develop their mother tongue? They hear it and imitate it. They are starting with sounds and moving onto words and then simple sentences. It is one of the miracles of human nature. When they are born, babies can make and hear every sound needed for all the world's languages. They arrive with the ability to use all these sounds called phonemes. Different languages use different phonemes, and babies learn to use the phonemes that belong to their language. There are three stages to this language developmental process.

Stage one: Learning sounds

By hearing the sounds, infants learn to process those that belong to their language and those that don't. This is known as phonemic awareness. The sound we make while admiring the baby, singing nursery rhymes, talking to the baby, and generally being verbal in their presence all goes to a good cause—phonemic awareness.

Stage two: Learning words

At this stage, the sounds the baby has heard are being put together to make words. These sounds *m-ah-m-ee* joined together are the sounds needed to say 'Mummy'. Often the early stage of stringing the sounds together results in simplified 'baby talk'. Ma-ma, da-da, and ba-ba are some examples. When I heard that magical sound for the first time, it was an absolute meltdown moment.

Stage three: Learning sentences

Now the words are strung into little sentences. Children begin to put the words they know into an order to make a sentence. There is a tremendous amount of development from this stage onwards. Learning tenses of verbs, building more vocabulary and, once school starts, learning to read and write. Language develops at an incredible rate. Each age and stage has milestones to reach the school readiness phase with language skills ready for school.

I checked up on the ages and stages and was pleased to see Kerry was doing well. What were those measures, and would we be able to keep up with our 'Look Who's Talking 2' member of the family? As parents, we were convinced our child was super-advanced, but it is important to realise children develop differently. Not every child reaches their milestones at the same pace.

Here's what I could expect from my child concerning language development.

EIGHT STAGES FROM BIRTH TO THREE YEARS TO REACH MEANINGFUL LANGUAGE AND COMMUNICATION.

1. At birth:

When newborn baby comes home, they can sense the rhythm of language. They can discern the pace and rise and fall of pitch in language.

2. From 4 to 6 months:

Infants begin to distinguish between a voice and other noises. They babble and cooing and sort out their noises to choose the sounds that belong to their particular language.

3. At 8 months:

Babies are recognising groups of sounds but are still learning their meaning. They are more likely to understand words related to their personal experiences. Food and their own body parts come at the top of the list.

4. When the baby reaches 12 months:

Now children can add meaning to words. They copy words you say, and their vocabulary grows and grows.\

5. At 18 months:

Children realise they need words to communicate. They are learning the difference between nouns and verbs. Nouns feature more than verbs.

6. **24 months to 2 years old:**

This is an exciting stage as children realise they can string words together to make a sentence. Short and sweet and usually about themselves is how these little sentences start. 'Me jump,' for example, is a bit of a selfish phrase and the beginning of speaking in sentences.

7. **From 30 to 36 months:**

Most of what children say at this stage is grammatically correct within their range of vocabulary. They make the occasional mistake with tenses, but with gentle correction, they soon learn how to change tense, use pronouns, and be more descriptive.

8. **Three years and older:**

As children grow, their language skills increase, and their vocabulary grows too. At the age of eleven or, maybe earlier, children have reached an adult language growth point. Their abstract concepts and what is known as 'concession' sentences, using 'although' or 'in spite of', is used more confidently as a pre-teen.

<u>Words of warning!</u>

I did remember reading about warning signs and possible speech delay. If there were any signs of lack of hearing or inability to make sounds, then a hearing test would be a good idea. Fortunately, Kerry did not show any signs of delay, and I was astounded at how quickly she learnt new words.

FINDING A TOOL TO HELP DEVELOP LANGUAGE.

A language development tool is the key to unlocking communication skills. The best tools I found came in the form of picture books. Making time to sit and look at Kerry's books and point out the different things she recognised was always a magical time. What fun we had together learning animal noises and nursery rhymes. Books are the best tool a parent can have to build up a child's vocabulary and interest in the world around them.

One of my favourite childhood authors is Dr Seuss. The way he brings fantasy into the home with *The Cat in the Hat* and all the rhyming words is a great way to encourage a young child to look at books. Pictures, text, and a simple story make these books wonderful to share with a toddler.

The cat arrives on a wet day and proceeds to turn the house upside down:

> *"We looked! And we saw him! The cat in the hat!*

> *And he said to us, "Why do you sit there like that?*

> *I know it is wet and the sun is not sunny.*

> *But we can have lots of good fun that is*
> *funny!"*

And they did with this beautiful story. *The Cat in the Hat* is full of crazy illustrations and catchy rhyming words. It was always a favourite in my home.

Books are the most beautiful way to communicate with your child. We had a tradition of bedtime stories. A much-loved time of the day when a book could tell a story, increase vocabulary, and help Kerry understand the world around her. Starting with simple health care stories and stories about animals as well as all the traditional fairy tales. There are so many picture storybooks to share with children as they grow up.

Pop-up books, puzzle books, sensory development books, flap books, board books, and cloth books. The selection is endless. Getting my child hooked on books was one of the smartest parenting moves I ever made.

Once I knew my child was listening to me and enjoying the books, not just for the pictures but also for the stories, our communication became more meaningful. We could laugh together over the funniest stories like Tasha Pym's, which asks if you have ever seen a Sneep? Or a Snook or perhaps a Floon? Listening to childish laughter is the best medicine I know!

Kerry was really enjoying her books, and some she knew so well she could recite the stories. I was so proud of her growing vocabulary. Looking at books and enjoying the stories was fantastic, but there is more to communication than words. Honest communication embraces empathy, body language, understanding and sharing feelings, relating a story, and communication through the written or printed word.

We used stories to talk about feelings and to learn how to empathise with the characters. The 'When I'm Feeling' series by Trace Moroney are lovely books to help children connect with their emotions. '1–2–3 My Feelings and Me' is a beautiful early-stage picture book about feelings too. And 'The Colour Monster' is another lovely discussion book as the monster relates his emotions to different colours. He is a very mixed-up monster, and the little girl in the story helps him sort out his feelings.

Animated TV shows, if you are very selective as a parent, can help little ones learn about empathy and kindness. I loved Maya the bee with her kindness, and being a busy bee made her a lovely role model. There are many suitable little shows for children. Sesame Street, with the Muppets, keeps everyone entertained. Puppets are a favourite teaching tool of mine. I had a basket of hand puppets for Kerry to play with. They make great spokespersons for feelings and acting out stories. Telling a story with a puppet on your hand is a lovely way to share the message. I found Kerry would talk to the puppet and sympathise with its troubles and difficulties.

I knew the need for good communication skills with my daughter would be extra crucial with another baby arriving soon. How would Kerry react to a new baby? I wondered if she would fully understand the implications of sharing her home with another family member. It was essential to show Kerry she was loved and important, not just with words but also with actions. I needed good communication techniques, and this little acronym seemed to help put a few simple tips into perspective:

V.E.R.B.A.L. = how to speak and show you are interested in talking to your child.

Here is how the VERBAL acronym works. Putting these points into practice really helped to focus on the way to communicate.

1. V—voice and
2. E—eye contact.
3. R—at the right level.
4. B—body language,
5. A—age-appropriate dialogue with
6. L—listening skills makes

.......perfect <u>verbal</u> communication.

<u>Voice</u>:

I knew from my teaching days and working with young children that tone of voice is fundamental with all ages of children. Babies will respond to calm, soothing voices and return coos and babbling sounds at the first communication stage. Shouting and sarcasm do not help in communication with young children. They shy away from harsh tones of voice, expecting punishment instead of empathy and understanding.

<u>Eye contact</u>:

Being sure to make eye contact is an integral part of communication. It shows that there is a connection and focus between the parties in the conversation. When eye contact is not clear, there is a sense of guilt or lack of concentration on the persons in the conversation.

Right level:

Finding the right level is important too. It is easy to see babies are usually in just the proper position for eye-to-eye conversation. There they are, right in front of you. I found getting down to a toddlers level more challenging. Playtimes and bedtimes were the best times for meaningful conversations. Then family mealtimes are another excellent opportunity to get down to the right level for communication. The whole family sitting around the table speaking about their day is an incredible time for sharing.

Body language:

Glaring, staring, gesticulating, and folding arms are all ways of sending different messages to different people. It is so tempting to fold those arms and look menacing. When I stood in an authoritative stance like that, I got no helpful information. Children may take the natural fight or flight response, which means, either way, communication breaks down, and a barrier is formed.

Age-appropriate dialogue:

Communication with a baby is all about connection through funny noises and choice of words. It may seem odd at first, but the purpose is to build up the sound base to introduce words later. Once the child has outgrown baby talk, the phrases become more sensible. Lots of repetition for this phase. I found it hard sometimes to tell Kerry's grandma that we needed to move away from some of the baby talk and offer Kerry some more adult words. Children get horribly teased at school if they are still using baby talk.

Listening skills:

I remember being told at school that you should listen twice as much as you speak because you have two ears and only one mouth. A pearl of wisdom passed on by a frustrated teacher with a class of girls who would never stop talking. However, it is a little reminder that listening is a significant part of communication. A good listener is sensitive to the emotions of others and their body language. A good listener turns off other distractions like cell phones and television programmes. A good listener is an active listener.

I found these do's and don'ts of active listening very useful. It is easy to make mistakes and not be a good listener when you are a busy parent.

Do...

• Let your child know you are listening with your body language.

• Repeat phrases to show you have been listening.

• Offer words of affirmation like 'really', 'I know,' and 'Wow!'

• Build on what your child has been saying with words of encouragement. Say things like, 'Wow, that is interesting! Tell me more about....'

• Watch your child's facial expressions for clues to how they are feeling.

Don't...

- Interrupt, even if a story is taking a long time. Try to interact, and then perhaps the story will reach a natural conclusion.

- Give the words needed all the time; let your child try to say what they need to say.

- Walk away or get busy with something else mid-conversation.

- Ignore your child when they are trying to get your attention. Instead, put them on hold while you finish what you are saying and then go back to their conversation as soon as you can.

My little toddler was growing up, and I was so pleased with her emergent independence. A favourite expression at this stage was 'me do!' She wanted to try and dress and brush her hair by herself. Potty training had gone well, and Kerry was going to a playgroup three mornings a week. I was getting some rest before baby number two arrived.

While I was resting at home one morning, putting my feet up after getting the nursery ready for the new baby, I came across an article in a mum's magazine. It was all about phrases parents use that can be misleading to their children. Kerry's little catchphrases were short and straightforward. I knew what they meant, and they were helping with communication. However, when I read some slogans parents use regularly, I decided to make a mental note to avoid them if I could.

Probably the most crucial phrase to avoid is the one that labels a child. I would be extra careful not to tell Kerry she was the cute child or the clever one, or the perfect one. No child should have to bear a label and try to live up to it.

I made a mental note to try not to use some of the others I read about. In fact, I remember my mum using some of these catchphrases, and I had definitely heard them at school.

'Practise makes perfect.'

That was one I had heard often. This phrase just gives a message of endless hard work and never achieving the goal. Perfection is an extremely <u>high level of achievement. Practise, yes, but with a level of manageable attainment.</u>

'You're OK.'

Instead of being reassuring, this phrase gives off the message that maybe the child is not OK, but they could be OK, well, they should be OK but... And therein lies a message of anxiety. There will always be occasions when children need a confidence boost, and finding words to empathise with their situation is far more reassuring than 'you're OK.'

'<u>Good job.</u>'

This becomes a catchphrase for everything. Sometimes parents need to look beyond the 'good job' and find out what was done. Use words of affirmation that highlight what the job was or what the skill was that helped to do good work.

'Don't talk to strangers.'

This is a critical phrase to look at realistically. We don't want our children talking to anyone who is not part of our circle of friends. However, in an emergency or if a child should get lost, finding the right person to talk to could make all the difference. Point out the people who help us by showing children what security guards or men and women in uniform look like. The checkout person in a shop or a mum with other children would be a safe option to go to for help.

Many other clichés suddenly became apparent to me, and I thought I would take more care about just using catchphrases without thinking what they meant.

COMMUNICATION WITH A TODDLER HAS ITS LIGHTER SIDE TOO.

Kerry often mispronounced words, and we laughed at the flutterbys (butterflies) in the garden and the haasgroppers (grasshoppers) hopping in the vegetables. Growing strawbabies (strawberries) was another favourite. Kerry mixed up her 's' sound with an 'f' sound, and when her favourite sweet, Smarties became Farties, my husband just thought that was the funniest thing he had ever heard.

He encouraged Kerry to share her 'Farties' with me. We laughed a great deal at her expense about Farties, especially as one of the things I seemed to crave during my pregnancy was sweets. Jelly babies, Smarties, and liquorice allsorts were all on the list.

It was going to be very important to have good communication skills before the new baby arrived. This was a big event. Kerry very sweetly put her head on my pregnant tummy to talk to the baby one day. A precious moment and I was able to explain that she was going to have a sister. Our next addition to the family was a girl.

'Did Mummy eat a big jelly baby?' asked Kerry as she tried to make sense of the fact that I was having a baby. She knew I was very fond of 'Farties,' so perhaps the baby came from the same sweetie counter. It was time to explain to Kerry that babies don't just come by eating jelly babies!

Milestone events and significant occasions often become what is known as teachable moments. The subject of my pregnancy and where the new baby comes from was a teachable moment. Psychology and child development did help with the factual knowledge but talking about sex can be embarrassing. I was glad that, as a family, we had kept lines of communication open. From an early age, we talked about different parts of the body using their proper names. It makes life easier in the long run. Keeping the subject of sexuality as natural as possible and explaining our differences was more accessible without a feeling of taboo.

Younger children enjoy looking at a picture book with you, and there are some excellent books explaining where babies come from. Some books comically deal with puberty, and that helps to relieve some of the embarrassment. We looked at a nature-based book showing how animals procreated, and the examples led up to human babies. Although we were just your regular mum, dad, and single child family, soon to be two children, we talked about how other babies can come into the world or become part of a family. Kerry nodded wisely and then said:

'So, I am not having a pink jelly baby sister,' and she laughed and ran off to play.

My husband and I exchanged glances too. We were glad she understood, and we left the book *What Makes a Baby* by Cory Silverberg on the table in the playroom, ready for other open discussions. I knew keeping an open and honest approach to matters relating to sex education would make this part of raising our daughter easier as she grew up.

Yes, making babies and sex education can be addressed in different ways. It is important to remember children are better off hearing about sex education, at whatever level they are at, from their parents. Starting early on, answering questions honestly and giving the right amount of information at the right level makes this part of parenting much easier and more acceptable for children who need to know they can discuss things with their parents.

The following suggestions to encourage talking about sex at different ages are helpful.

- **Early ages, pre-toddler:**
Using correct names for body parts is really important. Talking about exploring the body privately and not making the idea of finding out about aspects of the body shameful is an excellent way to start.

- **Ages 2 to 5 years:**

Helping children have a good idea of what is appropriate and what is not and setting boundaries is vital at this age. Make sure children know who is allowed to touch different body parts by setting boundaries.

Find 'teachable moments' to talk about what makes a baby. Use books like the ones written by Cory Silverberg. Embrace different family dynamics, so your child knows there are various family groups. Taper the amount of information according to your child's interest.

- **Ages 6 to 8 years:**

Our world and the world of our children has become a more prominent global space. Keeping children safe on the internet is particularly important. Explaining that bodies and body parts are private is a crucial factor. If there is an opportunity to talk about the differences between boys and girls, make it a gender-neutral kind of talk. Always answer questions with honesty.

- **Ages 9 to 12 years:**

The pre-teens and some little girls may be starting to show signs of puberty. This is an excellent time to check in about feelings. Do pre-teens know how to manage emotions and changes in hormones? Once again, open communication is essential.

- **Teenagers:**

The age of emotions, puberty, and mixing with the opposite sex, coming straight out the pre-teens when opposite gender mixing was avoided. Now there is an interest in the opposite sex. Paving the way all along the route of growing up will make all the difference at this stage. Conversations about safe sex and safety on the internet will make safety the key for all sex-related discussions.

A VITAL FACTOR OF ANY FORM OF COMMUNICATION IS EMPATHY.

Barack Obama had these wise words to say about empathy:

> *'Learning to stand in somebody else's shoes, to see through their eyes, that's how peace begins. And it's up to you to make that happen. Empathy is a quality of character that can change the world.'*

C. JoyBell C., author of books and poetry, puts this concept into words children can understand and says:

> *'Empathy is the ability to step outside of your own bubble and into the bubbles of other people.'*

Communication with children gets more complicated as they grow older. Therefore, psychologists recommend that opening those doors of communication needs to start early.

Children go through a phase of asking 'why' often. This can be a challenging time and requires every last ounce of patience you may have. Did you know children ask about 40,000 questions between the ages of two and five? That is a lot of questions, and parents need to try and answer them because every answer you give helps your child learn something.

Many questions can seem ridiculous, but usually, when children are given a good answer, the problem ceases. Why then do children ask so many questions?

Here are some explanations:

A need to know about this subject:

Some questions can be challenging but try your best to answer, and when in doubt—well, there is always Google!

Attention seeking:

If you are getting endless questions, perhaps your child just wants some quality time with you. Take a break and spend some time chatting and answering questions. This is an opportunity to see if your child can come up with a sensible answer, and then you can discuss the topic together.

Defiance:

Sometimes children just want to challenge you, the parent, and question everything you ask them to do. This can be very frustrating, especially at bedtime, when endless questions arise about the bedtime routine. 'Why must I brush my teeth? Why must I wash my face?' and so on. The temptation is to say, 'Because I said so,' but in order to keep communication lines open, give a sensible answer. That should end the questions until next time.

My family was growing. I had questions of my own. How would I cope with two children? Was it challenging to go back to the infant phase again? How would the new baby affect Kerry? It was an exciting thought to have a new baby arriving soon.

I took a deep breath and reminded myself of the lovely gentle poem.

Desiderata.

Such beautiful, peaceful words. Words for life.

> *'Go placidly amid the noise and the haste,*

> *And remember what peace there may be in silence.*

> *As far as possible, without surrender,*

> *Be on good terms with all persons.*

> *Speak your truth quietly and clearly,*

> *And listen to others….'*

It is a beautiful reminder of keeping peace in your communication with others and, in the noise and haste of life, to remember to listen to others.

CHAPTER FOUR

DECIDING ON DISCIPLINE DELIVERY AND THE BASICS OF BOUNDARIES

D rum roll and clash of cymbals, and our second daughter made a grand entrance. She made us wait for two weeks over her due date, and after jokes about giving birth to an elephant, I was relieved that her big day finally arrived. Kerry was so excited to have a baby sister and spent hours sorting bootees, laying out all the bath-time toys, and getting the crib ready.

We called the new baby Nikki. A decisive name meaning 'victory'. Little did we know at the time that this little one was going to push our boundaries, and we would have to be strong in our parenting skills to be the ones winning the battles. Nikki turned our lives upside down from the day she arrived home. A little ball of fire who did not like the idea of sleep and needed so much attention.

I was reminded of a game I used to play with my family. Boys loved this game because it was all about armies and winning battles. The game, called *Risk*, used strategy to protect boundaries. Countries were defeated, and battles raged through the roll of the dice. I did not want my home to become a war zone and found I was losing the battle with two children.

Boundaries. That was what we would need as a family—boundaries for the parents and limitations for the children. While Nikki was still young, I began to think about limits and how to set them. Every general must be ready for battle, I thought, and I wanted to be sure I was prepared to defend my boundary.

Before I could set a boundary, I had to know more about this as a parenting concept.

What are boundaries? In relationships, they define what makes you feel comfortable within yourself and how you would like to be treated. It is about healthy communication and positive self-esteem. A boundary sets a healthy dividing line between our needs and wants and those of our children.

These three simple points sum up setting boundaries in a quick and uncomplicated way:

1. There must be clear expectations of what the boundary will deliver.

2. The parties involved must communicate clearly to avoid mixed messages.

3. In the process of observing the boundary, there are choices followed by consequences.

In simple terms, it is what you want, how you want it done, and what will happen if you are not following the rules for observing the boundary.

While I wondered how this would work for a toddler and a new baby, an opportunity arose to set a simple boundary. I had to admit that the new baby was demanding. Utterly different to Kerry. This little one was fussy, restless, and had colic. Getting her to settle took a good deal of my time, and I could see Kerry was feeling the stress of this new sibling. The baby was still in her crib and sleeping in the main bedroom. The cot and the nursery things were in the nursery that Kerry had used. She had happily handed over all her stuff for her new sister. Well, that was before this new bundle arrived.

One morning I could not find Kerry anywhere. I heard some funny wailing noises from the nursery. Not Nikki, but then what or who? I rushed into the nursery to find Kerry lying in the cot wearing a rather odd-looking diaper and a vest. She was making funny gaga noises and wanting a bottle. I was shocked. Was this my toddler? Talking the baby talk and wanting a bottle. Then I realised what this was all about. Kerry thought if she acted like a baby, she would get my attention. She had regressed to her baby behaviour. I tried to talk to her, but she kept up the baby talk.

At that moment, I knew I needed my toddler back and not another baby. I decided to go along with her 'game' and brought her the bottle. When she had finished, she wanted to get out of the cot. I shook my head and explained there were consequences. If she chose to be a baby, she would be treated like one and would have to stay in the cot like a baby.

I left the nursery, wondering if I had done the right thing. An hour later, a quiet voice came from the nursery.

'Mummy, can I be a big girl now?' said Kerry.

> *'Of course you can,'* I said as I lifted her out of the cot.

We sat down there and then in the nursery, and I explained the boundary of being a helper and how a big sister can behave. I promised from my side of the border to spend more time with Kerry when the baby was asleep or when we could do something together, like visit our neighbours. I said big sisters get to spend extra time with their daddy, which made her happy. When my husband came home, we spoke about setting boundaries so the whole family would benefit and how these boundaries would need to be revisited as the girls grew up.

I went to bed that night with one foot out of bed, rocking the pram but feeling a lot better about our family and how we would work together, setting our boundaries. It was going to take teamwork and consistent guidelines to overcome the challenge of this new baby. I really felt I was in the deep end with Nikki, who was so different from our first daughter.

The next day, still feeling a little bleary-eyed from interrupted sleep, I had a call from my mum. She offered to come over and sit with the girls so my husband and I could go out for coffee.

> *'You two need a break. I'll watch the girls, and you take some time out,'* said Mum.

I was so grateful. I made Mum promise to call if Nikki became hysterical and gave Kerry a hasty kiss goodbye before Mum changed her mind or the baby woke up. There was a cosy coffee shop down the road. I tucked a notebook in my bag, and my husband and I set off down the road for some time out.

We enjoyed our coffee, and the phone had not rung yet. I thought I would see if my husband would talk about setting boundaries. I decided to tackle the subject like a business venture. It seemed like a way he would understand, using office-type buzzwords. These came to mind.

- Goal setting.
- Mission statement.
- Going in for the deep dive.
- Micro-influencer.

I thought a quick play on words might just get my husband's attention.

I waited for him to finish his waffle and ice cream before taking out my notebook and pen. He looked at me a bit quizzically, and I smiled.

> *'Honey,'* I said. *'Are you ready to go in for the deep dive?'*

I could see I had his attention, so I continued with my office jargon.

> *'I think we should do some goal setting and come up with a mission statement,'* I said.

I was trying to keep a straight face. I was now speaking his kind of language. He nodded, but I could see he was not quite sure what I had in mind.

'I think we need to set goals for our family. Now we have a micro-influencer; perhaps some synergy will help us move forward,' I added, and I saw him smile.

Yes, I had his attention now!

It was the right time to discuss setting boundaries, no matter how small they were. Suppose we start the way we plan to continue. In that case, raising a family in this day and age could be a lot easier—boundaries we could revisit and limitations that would help us with discipline and family values.

We spent a while getting our values together, and that made setting the goals more manageable.

This was our simple formula and starting point. There are so many family values, but the five that seemed to resonate well with our family were: respect, honesty, patience, kindness, responsibility, and courage.

I scrunched up my nose at the last one my hubby chose. Courage? Yes, he felt courage was a significant value. It takes courage to hold to values and what you believe in. Winston Churchill said this about the family and the home, and he was a man of courage:

'There is no doubt that it is around the family and the home that all the greatest virtues, the most dominating virtues of human, are created, strengthened, and maintained.'

I had to agree with my husband that courage was a family value or virtue, and judging by our little micro-influencer, we needed courage. Courage to stand by our family values and courage to believe in the bond we would share through the good times and the tough ones.

We finished the last sips of our coffee and went home to rescue Mum from the demands of the two little people we had brought into this world. I felt very encouraged by our time out, and now there was a clear way forward to setting boundaries. How were we going to implement these family values and share these ideas with our girls?

'Sharing is caring is such a cliché these days, but the idea seemed to fit for putting together family values and setting boundaries. How could we all get together to share these values and put some boundaries in place? My mum used to share family discussions at the dinner table. Sitting together at mealtimes was an integral part of the family structure. Once we had our basic family blueprint, we needed a way to get this across to our children so they would grow up respecting the values we had chosen.

This was my 3D approach to setting the boundaries through the values, and then it was going to be a shared discussion point at mealtimes or whenever there was a need for discipline.

The 3D dynamic to implement family values… Define, Discuss and Develop.

Define –What parents feel are their personal family values.

<u>Discuss</u>—How the values and boundaries are explained to the children.

<u>Develop</u>—When the values and boundaries need updating as family dynamics change.

Our defined family values were:

- Respect
- Honesty
- Patience
- Kindness
- Responsibility
- Courage

I decided to make a chart with these words, pin it up in the children's rooms, and print one for the kitchen. Kerry thought it was hilarious that I put one in the nursery. I explained the need for everyone to know about our values and that Nikki would be looking up to her big sister at first as they grew up together.

Kerry made a funny face. I could see she felt this noisy little sibling would never be able to grow up and be responsible. It was rewarding, though, to see Kerry was beginning to understand some of the values. Respect is always a difficult concept for children, but if they grow up with respect in their home, they begin to see how it works.

Once I had made the chart, I decided to spend some time on Kerry's first value. Respect, I explained in four-year-old terms, was looking after things and caring about other people, not just yourself.

> *'Mummy and Daddy respect each other, and we want our children to do the same,'* I explained to Kerry.

We went through the other values together, and then I asked her if she understood what we were talking about.

> *'Yes, it's like when Daddy opens the car door for Mummy. That's respect and being kind too,'* she said, and I nodded.

> Then she added, *'Daddy is patient too because he has to wait while Mummy remembers to get her phone, then her shopping list, and then her cardigan,'* Kerry smiled at me.

> *'And he is responsible for the car, and he is a courageous driver,'* I added since we were making good use of the car as a role model for our family values.

It was a worthwhile discussion, and we shared the ideas at the supper table. Kerry was propped up on a cushion, looking very important, and her baby sister was in her pram's sitting position. Not ready for table talk, but she seemed happier being with us in the midst of the family gathering. I was hoping her colic and cramping days were over.

As we sat around the table, I was reminded of a quote from Michael J. Fox:

'Family is not an important thing. It's everything!'

Now we had the values, and we set the boundaries according to the family needs. Right now, with a new baby and a little explorer, the limits would be about safety and taking care of simple things like toys and books. Getting Kerry involved with keeping her room tidy and helping with a few minor tasks like setting the table was a start to responsibility. Nikki was still an infant, but her time would come.

The children needed to respect their parents by engaging with them and understanding why they could or could not do certain things. There had to be consequences because, without a consequence, there is no boundary. I read about consequences being the combination of love and limitations. Love is there to teach children how to respect their limits and restrictions, in the form of a consequence, are to keep the boundary in place. Regulation takes away a privilege, for example. At a young age, this could be missing a treat or having to go to bed early.

Kerry learned the love and limitations concept very quickly. She wanted to please her parents and was relatively easygoing with a gentle nature. Getting down to her level of understanding was easy. Kerry was a creative child. One day there was an incident that brought several boundaries into play. Encouraged by her younger, more mischievous sister, she decided to decorate a wall in her bedroom with a collage. The trouble was, one of my treasured magazines was used to provide the pictures, and toothpaste had acted as the glue to stick the photos on the wall. The result was a very sticky, gooey mess. I walked into the bedroom as the house seemed noticeably quiet. Unusually quiet. When I saw the mess on the wall, I shouted out very loudly,

'What on earth is going on in here?' I was furious.

Several boundaries were crossed with this one incident.

- Making a mess in the bedroom.
- Taking things that did not belong to the girls, aka Mum's special fashion mag.
- Hiding from the truth.

Yes, when I discovered the awful mess, the girls ran and hid in the cupboard. A loud sneeze from Nikki revealed their hiding place.

It was time to talk about boundaries. Nikki was a bit older, and Kerry was definitely old enough to know what she did was wrong.

The girls were called out of the cupboard, and with their heads held low, I sat them down next to me, and we had a good talk about what was wrong with their actions. I made sure my communication with them was clear, on their level, and I gave them the consequences of their actions.

We dealt with each of the boundaries they had crossed.

- <u>Messing up the wall in the bedroom</u>: I had to stifle a small smile as I realised Kerry and Nikki were trying to be creative, and I knew I had been busy this last week. They would have to clean the wall and use their pocket money to buy me another magazine.
- <u>Taking things that do not belong to you</u>: This was a necessary boundary and crossed our family value of respect. The girls looked wide-eyed when I explained that it was wrong to go into my bedroom and take the magazine that belonged to me.

'We did knock knock, but you did not answer,' said Nikki.

I nodded and reminded the girls that no answer meant no entry.

• <u>Hiding from the truth:</u> The cupboard hideaway became a family joke later, but at the time, I made this a serious part of our boundaries. We do not hide from the truth.

The girls had to face the consequences of their actions. It was an excellent opportunity to discuss boundaries with them and later with my husband. How were we handling boundaries with our girls? I read about some very encouraging guidelines, and I felt I had followed these to reach a positive outcome.

Golden rules for setting and following through with boundaries were simple. I made five of them:

1. Keep calm throughout the transgression of crossing a boundary.

2. Be unemotional and don't overreact to the incident.

3. Exercise patience to talk through what has made you upset.

4. Always follow through on a boundary. If there is no consequence or follow-through, there is no boundary.

5. Offer sympathy and comfort to the transgressors, but do not back down or give in to the boundary.

When my husband came home, we sat down and discussed the incident. Had I covered the outcomes of the boundary issue correctly? Healthy boundaries had to result in a positive effect in keeping with our goal to raise great children. We went through our healthy boundaries checklist and came up with a score of 8/10; there were some flaws. We were not perfect parents, but ready, willing, and able to try our best. We went through the list and worked out the score.

TEN HEALTHY BOUNDARIES FOR PARENTS

1. Never be physical in confronting your children.

2. Manage the issues in a timely manner.

3. Let your boundaries and consequences go hand in hand.

4. Make boundaries to keep children safe and disciplined.

5. Be consistent with the consequences.

6. Keep body language and tone of voice neutral.

7. Do not let your children's emotions get the better of you.

8. Get directly to the point—what are the issues or crossed boundaries.

9. Link the offence to your family values.

10. When there is an opportunity, reward good behaviour.

How did I score? Honestly, not a 10/10! I had failed on point 6 with my outburst of emotion when I saw the mess that made the girls before they scuttled into the cupboard. Then I had nearly let Nikki's tearful face get to me! I realised she was very good at dramatics and persuasion, and I overcame my feelings of pity regarding strong discipline preference.

The end result was an opportunity to set our boundaries, implement them and complement the girls for their cleaning up. The next day I bought a big piece of paper for each of them, and they made collages out of some old magazines Mum was throwing out and glue sticks bought from the stationery store.

It was a win-win situation as the children saw a love-based boundary reaction instead of a fear-based response that could have been the result if we had no boundaries for our girls. They both made lovely collages dedicated to the things Mummy and Daddy love. I could see they were beginning to appreciate their parents as, under Kerry's guidance, Nikki cut out, somewhat haphazardly, pictures of roses and puppies, beautiful scenery for me, and golf courses and chocolates for her dad.

That evening at the dinner table, we acknowledged the girl's wise choices and how they handled their punishment. We had a good laugh about the idea of hiding in the cupboard.

> *'Mummy is a super detective. She always finds out everything,'* said Kerry.

> *'Special agent Lovemore,'* said my husband. The girls had a good laugh at the joke...

CHAPTER FIVE

SHIFTING AGGRESSIVE BEHAVIOUR TO BE IN YOUR FAVOUR

I t was amazing how the time flew by. Suddenly we were through the infant phase with two little ones, and Nikki was at a little playschool close to Kerry's big school. Three mornings a week, I had some time to pursue my hobbies. I joined a pottery class and enjoyed moulding clay into something for the house. Pots and jugs and all sorts of different clay objects filled all kinds of nooks and crannies in our tiny home.

Kerry loved her school. After her first week of finding her feet, her confidence grew, and she delighted in learning to read and bringing home books to share. I decided to volunteer to help in the library, and that filled up another morning for me. I could see how much Kerry enjoyed having her mum at school, and I loved being in the library too. A win-win situation for both of us.

Nikki was another story. I kept wondering how two girls from the same parents could be so different. Nikki was often in trouble for assertive behaviour, and sometimes, when I went to fetch her, she was sitting in the secretary's office looking like a thunder cloud. Trying to talk to Nikki was almost impossible. It was always somebody else's fault. She found herself in trouble, and according to Nikki, there were no teachers that liked her.

The school was not her favourite place, and the system seemed to be her enemy.

How were we going to deal with this 'angry bird'? She had kept us awake as a baby and had been so active as a toddler. What was causing her anger at school? Well, just playschool at this stage. How were we going to deal with this troublesome child?

We had taken Nikki to see a paediatrician when she was very little and would not stop crying. He suggested that our baby was frustrated, and once she started walking, she would stop crying and move and explore. Her moods did improve marginally, but this little girl was still very frustrated. I decided to look at my notes from my child psychology classes. There I found ten causes of aggressive behaviour. I wondered how many would apply to our daughter. Were any of these ten causes the reason for her aggressive behaviour?

I went through the list:

- Injury
- Psychosis
- Trauma
- Mood disorder
- Frustration
- Family structure
- Relationships with others
- Impulsivity
- Life experiences
- Conduct disorder

This list of reasons for aggressive behaviour did seem radical, but I needed to understand if any of these behaviours could be part of my child's motivation for aggression. I wanted to be open-minded and not minimise any of her actions if there could be some reasons for her unwanted behaviours. I reviewed each topic carefully.

Injury:

She had the usual energetic tumbles and scraped knees but no injury that would account for aggressive behaviour. A head injury or accident-causing anxiety would account for this kind of behaviour. I felt I could safely cross this one off the list.

Psychosis:

This got a definite 'no' reaction from me. Nikki may be a bit impulsive sometimes and look disturbed, but she was not psychotic. She may have driven her parents to a state of psychosis, but I was sure that was not her intention. There was an underlying sweetness to Nikki, and her love of nature and collecting bugs in boxes was quite endearing. Well, until the creepies crawled out, that is!

Trauma:

There were no real signs of trauma in Nikki's life. Her family was supportive. She had a big sister to be with when they were home together. A year or so ago, moving house with two children had been traumatic, but Nikki had loved eating takeout food on the floor while everything was unpacked. This did not seem to be a reason for aggressive behaviour.

Mood disorder:

There were some pretty dramatic mood swings mentioned under the category of mood disorder—children who may be bipolar or have other forms of depression, leading to aggressive outbursts. Nikki could be irritable and impulsive if she did not get her way. Did that put her in the mood disorder category? No, I did not think so and was relieved to cross that off the list.

Frustration:

Yes, this was definitely an attribute I could attach to my child. However, was it the usual frustration of a child who can't find the words to express themselves or the lack of fine motor skills to complete the tasks they wanted to do? I felt the frustration level was probably higher than average, and Nikki wanted to do more advanced puzzles or build something clever with her Lego. Getting the right pieces together and the item finished with her short span of concentration was frustrating. She wanted to keep up with her sister. I put frustration into my basket of options.

Family structure:

I looked at the effect our family structure could have on Nikki. Our family seemed pretty normal and uncomplicated. Then I pressed pause in the day to day running of our household and had a second look. Perhaps there was a problem with some sibling rivalry. There was an age gap of nearly four years. Kerry was doing so well at everything. Teachers loved her; she had lovely friends and was excelling at everything. Due to the age gap, Kerry was the first to do many things in our family. She would always be one step ahead of Nikki. That was a fact of life. I could not change that, but I realised that if this were a problem in Nikki's mind, I could make it less noticeable. Family structure was something I would have to look at concerning my youngest daughter's aggression.

Relationships with others:

Every parent wants their child to have good relationships with others. I was no different. Seeing my girls laughing and playing with friends was always a happy moment. I did notice that Nikki liked to play with younger children. When I arrived to fetch her, she was always with the group below hers running around the playground. Nikki felt more comfortable with younger children. She loved visiting her cousins because they were younger than she was.

Impulsivity:

Making sudden decisions or being part of disruptive behaviour was something I could attribute to Nikki. She was overexcitable and did not consider the consequences of her actions. Jumping up at inappropriate times, calling out before anyone else had a turn, and making poor decisions were all part of Nikki's lifestyle. She did silly things sometimes and could be exhausting with her enthusiasm. There were definite signs of ADHD impulsive behaviour. Could this be the explanation I was looking for?

Life experiences:

I tried hard to think of any significant life experiences that could affect my child's behaviour. She was the youngest and had always had plenty of attention. There were no considerable life-changing experiences I could think of. I did notice she was susceptible to certain things. A trip to town on a bus and the hooter's loud sound made her cover her ears. A new t-shirt with a scratchy label drove her mad until we cut the tag off. When grandpa came to dinner and chewed rather loudly, she left the table in a hurry. Nikki might have sensory processing difficulties, leading to a fight or flight response.

Conduct Disorder:

Conduct disorder, or CD, is described as hostile and violent behaviour. The sheer severity of this disorder with abusive behaviour made me shudder. I knew there were children with these symptoms, but Nikki was not one of them. A child who delicately nurtured bugs and eased caterpillars back to their leaves was not going to have a conduct disorder. We did not always like her conduct, but as parents, we would find out why Nikki struggled to make friends her own age and settle in at school.

I reviewed my list and saw I could tick five out of the ten listed causes.

- Frustration
- Family structure
- Being impulsive
- Relationships
- Life experiences (with others)

Now that I had identified the main culprits of my child's aggressive behaviour, I needed to address them individually and get to the root of the problem. I had not experienced any of this with Kerry. I knew these behaviours existed, and I had heard other mothers speak about them. It was my turn to step up and deal with these issues before they became entrenched and regular behaviours.

I looked for ways to help Nikki with those areas that may be troubling her and causing aggressive behaviour.

Frustration can be helped through learning how to express feelings. When she would get angry because she could not reach a toy, I explained the surface and helped her to acquire the toy.

The family structure would be different for every family, but I began to see how Kerry was set on a pedestal in our situation. Kerry won prizes at school; Kerry loved dancing and singing; Kerry was confident and had good interpersonal skills. My mum loved Kerry, and they had a great connection with each other. Kerry was the first grandchild, so there had been a lot of fuss made over her arrival. Mum loved sewing and started to make the girls dresses. There was always a dress for Kerry and another little outfit for Nikki.

> *'I just had some scraps left, so I made this little outfit for Nikki Noo,'* said Mum.

The thought was genuinely kind, and the nickname I knew Mum was just trying to have an endearing name for Nikki. However, I felt this made Nikki feel like second best with the family structure being an issue. I had a kindly chat with my mum, and she agreed. Matching dresses for the two girls was not the best idea now. Nikki was growing up and needed her own identity. Added to that, Nikki Noo was very babyish. Noo was growing up. At school, she was known as Nix, and we decided to encourage Nix as her nickname. The next time Mum came round with some sewing, she had made summer shorts for the girls with sunhats to go with the new outfits. Each set was completely different. I thanked Mum when the girls were out of earshot. Nikki loved her new shorts but refused to wear the hat. I smiled, half the battle had been won, and that was enough for the time being.

Impulsivity is a challenge. Young children can be impulsive, often because they have not listened to the instructions carefully.

Ask children to repeat what it is you have said. When they repeat the instruction, you will know they better grasp what they should be doing. Help the impulsive child with problem-solving skills. Let them know there is more than one way to do something, and they can always ask for help. Talk about structure and safety. Have some house rules that have to be observed for everyone's health and safety. Code of conduct outside the house helps impulsive children obey the rules inside and outside. Reward good behaviour and be a good role model yourself.

Relationships are an essential factor in life. In our society today, everyone has to relate to others and build relationships that are positive socially and emotionally.

Nikki's daycare teacher had some good suggestions to help Nikki with her interpersonal skills. I made a note of these to share with the family:

• Have some playtime together, and keep connected through the game.

• Involve Nikki in some household chores and do the work together.

• Show an interest in whatever she is doing.

• Talk about and share feelings for each other and friends, creating empathy for others.

• Encourage playdates with other children.

• Have less TV time and more time together with family members or friends.

These suggestions all seemed like easy and practical ways to build relationships, and I was sure they would work.

<u>Life experiences</u> are such a vital part of moulding our children. Do they have happy memories of their childhood, or has some irrational behaviour made life difficult? I knew that I needed to sort out Nikki's sensory issues. If I could help her overcome them, she would enjoy parties and holidays and play with friends. There were many other social occasions that children wanted to add to their memory bank. The first day at school, playing with a pet, favourite toys, and stories. All these life experiences needed to be joyful for both the girls. I realised that they needed their own memories.

Watching Kerry get ready with great excitement for her ballet classes while Nikki was reluctantly getting her leotard together made me realise that there was another area where the girls needed different extramural activities. I was walking past the gym room at the school one day and heard some loud shouts. I looked in the window and saw a whole bunch of energetic children having karate lessons. It was physical, active, noisy, and lively. What caught my attention was there were boys and girls in the class.

> *'I think I have found something for Nikki to do instead of ballet,'* I said to my husband that evening.

He looked at me sideways and waited for the suggestion to come from me.

'Karate. I think Nikki would love karate, and it would be a good life experience for her,' I added.

The next day, when I went to collect Nikki from her class, we took a walk past the karate lesson together. She peeped around the doorway, and Sensei, the karate teacher, welcomed Nikki to the class. Karate was so different from ballet, and Nikki loved the idea of doing karate. The leotard was swapped in favour of the karate gear. Nikki loved her karate lessons and had a new sense of independence with growing confidence.

Birthday parties were another area I learned could be different. It was more work and planning, but each child chose their own theme, and the food decor and activities suited the theme. It was bugs for Nikki with a long caterpillar cake. Kerry chose a fairy princess party. All her friends were in the ballet group, so everyone loved the masses of tulle and pink party food.

It was through respecting their differences I could see how the family dynamics were improving. The girls were allowed to decorate their own rooms. One holiday we spent time as a family decorating a pink pink pink bedroom for Kerry and a wild green bedroom for Nikki. The girls chose their own lamps and wall decals. Kerry had ballet dancers everywhere, and Nikki wanted bright red ladybirds to brighten up her crazy green room.

'It's my greenhouse,' she announced proudly.

Then, to finish off their rooms, they designed their own door signs. This was another opportunity to talk about boundaries and what it meant to have your own space and identity. There were responsibilities attached to having your room. Keep it tidy and make your own bed. Always putting books away neatly and toys and games too. Nikki wanted to add a giant skull and crossbones signs and 'Danger—Keep Out' notices to scare off any intruders. It was hard to convince her that it is unnecessary to barricade your room; setting boundaries is about setting a good example of how you want to be respected by other people. I tried to explain that slamming doors and shouting out did not set a sensible boundary but one of anger. I could see Kerry understood this as she was older. It would take some perseverance and time to help Nikki understand the concept.

I wondered how I would help the girls understand the concept of honouring everyone's personal space. A quote from Mahatma Gandhi helped me with this problem, he said:

> *'An ounce of practice is worth more than tons of preaching.'*

That idea resonated well, and I put a door sign on our bedroom too. A simple gesture to say three things. I thought these things would help the girls respect our privacy and the values we were trying to create in our home. Our door sign said:

- Knock before entering.
- Always bring a smile with you.
- Remember, peace and harmony live here.

Our girls loved the idea that we had a door sign too. The very next day, there was a knock on the door. It was Saturday, and there was no school to be rushing off to first thing in the morning. Kerry and Nikki waited politely for the 'come in' reply. The two of them entered with a tray of coffee and cookies and with two big smiles on their faces. That was reassuring, and I knew they had grasped something behind our door sign.

We added a desk and study corner for Kerry. Nikki would get her study corner when she was given written homework. We talked about how important it was to have a quiet place to study and respect the person learning and their need for peace and quiet. Nikki was smiling, and I knew that wicked little grin of hers. She wanted to know about knocking on Kerry's door, and I said that was important too. The next thing Nikki started was one of her jokes. She launched into a series of 'knock-knock' jokes to tie in with the idea that we should knock on doors. Nikki loved to tell a funny jokes.

'Knock knock,' said Nikki.

We all raised our eyebrows and answered,

'Who's there?'

'Kerry,' she answered.

'Kerry, who?' we kept in joke mode.

'Kerry, on with your homework.'

Everyone laughed at that one, but it did show me that something about personal space was beginning to sink in.

Our family dinners were going well, and we took time at these meals to have an appreciation day once a week. It was our Thanksgiving Thursday. On Thursdays, everyone around the table said something about the family they appreciated. I thought about my family as we were growing into the next phase at school and dealing with new problems. Yes, Nikki was still a difficult child, but with boundaries in place and an appreciation of her different nature and individuality, we handled the situation with her outburst in a more controlled and consistent manner. Kerry was moving up the ladder of success at primary school, and the principal had invited me to get more involved in the preliminary phase.

The school librarian had seen how passionate I was about books and reading. She knew I had counselling skills as well as my educational skills. After an incident in the library involving aggressive behaviour from one of the younger children, she had approached the principal to ask if he would consider hiring me on a part-time basis.

> *'You would be an asset to the school. You have a great way with the younger children. With your background in counselling and developmental psychology, you could help parents and teachers overcome problems with some of the difficult children,'* said Shirley Robson.

I was thrilled at the idea of being employed again and doing the work I loved.

The thought of being back in a school environment, even if it was only a part-time capacity, was exciting. I wanted involvement with these young lives using my skills and experience as a mother and an educator.

This quote from Plato reminded me of my purpose:

'No man should bring children into the
world who is unwilling to persevere to
the end in their nature and education.'

The stage was set for me to be part of the school and to use my skills to help where I could with the aim of persevering with children's nature and their education: nature and nurture.

Chapter Six

Preparing for When School Isn't Cool

I enjoyed being part of the school. The girls were doing well. Although Nikki said, none of the teachers liked her! It was a pattern I would have to get used to. She was still managing her work, and Kerry was excelling. I looked forward to my library mornings and helping with the younger children and their reading programmes. It was great to put my teaching skills into practice again.

One morning I walked into the library to see an overly concerned teacher sitting at her desk with her head held low. I thought I detected a tear, but she wiped it away as I came into the library.

> *'What's wrong?'* I asked as I saw her holding something that looked like a dagger on the desk.

The librarian showed me the 'dagger' made out of a broken plastic ruler. I was shocked. How did something like this get into our school? I waited patiently for a moment while the librarian gathered her senses and told me about the weapon.

She had confiscated it from one of the little boys in first grade. I raised my eyebrows as I realised how young the children in this grade were. A troubled child, no doubt. Something serious must trigger wanting to use this dangerous weapon at school. The shocking part was that the little boy had made the dagger. He had pre-meditated utilising this weapon. Coloured with a red pencil at the tip to represent blood and with a handle wrapped in coloured tape. This made a deliberate statement of intended violence.

I sat down with the librarian, and I went through some possible causes of violent behaviour. Reaching into the developmental psychology knowledge I had, I tried to develop possible reasons for this aggressive behaviour. There had to be a motivation behind this little boy's feelings of anger. We went through the list of possibilities, and I suggested his class teacher join us for a round table discussion before taking our findings to the headmaster.

These possible reasons came from a list of 8 things that could lead to aggressive behaviour in children:

1. A victim of physical or sexual abuse.

2. Being bullied at home or school.

3. Media, negative influences through watching violent movies.

4. Exposure to violence in the home environment.

5. Drug or alcohol abuse.

6. Stressful family issues.

7. Brain damage.

8. Genetic predisposition to violence.

I chaired a discussion between the class teacher and the librarian. Some interesting, although emotional issues, came to the fore. An abusive father and an unstable home environment. Aggression at home was expected in this child's life—a frustrated little boy bringing his emotional attention-seeking to school. I felt I had helped the librarian, my friend Shirley, to see it was not her fault, and his teacher had a better idea of how to handle this boy in her class.

The next day I was called to the headmaster's office! It was a strange feeling being called to the headmaster's office, one that possibly never goes away from your school days. I stood there, wondering if I was in trouble. Did I talk out of turn with my counselling? I knocked on the door and waited.

'*Come in,*' came the deep voice of the principal of the school, Mr Boardman. He reached out his hand and shook mine.

'*Do take a seat, Mrs Lovemore,*' he said.

I sat down, feeling nervous.

Perhaps I overstepped the mark in the library with counselling advice.

'Mrs Lovemore,' began the principal, very formally. *'Mrs Robson, in the library, was telling me about your professional insight into the situation she experienced recently with one of our troublesome first-grade boys.'*

I waited for some sort of objection to interfering, but Mr Boardman was incredibly grateful for my help with the situation on that day. He asked if I would like to join the staff in a part-time capacity. I was thrilled at the idea of being more involved in the school and using my professional experience. I would be helping in the library and offering counselling skills and workshops for teachers and parents. Mr Boardman introduced me formally to the staff at the next staff meeting, and the secretary included a paragraph about my skills in the school newsletter.

My husband was excited. He knew I was keen to be involved in a professional capacity. Kerry was proud to have her mum at school, sitting with all the teachers. Nikki looked wide-eyed at me and said,

'Are you a teacher now, Mummy? Will you give me extra homework and more spelling to learn?'

Poor Nikki, afraid of extra work from school, saw me as part of the 'enemy'. I assured her I was there to help teachers and children if they had problems. She nodded seriously.

Nikki proceeded to tell us about a little girl in her class who had 'embossed eyes', and we all listened very carefully to her explanation of this problem. There was a little girl in her class who wore very thick lenses in her glasses. Although it was an amusing use of words, we as parents and teachers had to encourage children to empathise with others who struggled with disabilities.

There would be no shortage of ideas for workshops to help teachers, parents, and children with school issues. I helped Nikki understand that embossed eyes, or crossed eyes, were being supported by the glasses. This little girl needed to feel accepted at school by everyone.

'Oh, like the ants in my pants!' added Nikki.

We laughed at that comment as a family, but I realised then that my child had her share of problems, and I did not want her to be labelled as the class clown because she could not sit still.

Mr Boardman asked me to address the staff at the next staff meeting about my school role and ask for future workshops and staff team building ideas. I felt very well received by everyone and asked for suggestions for relevant topics.

These were the most prominent areas of concern.

- Bullying
- Peer pressure and resolving conflict
- Addictions

- Academic difficulties and disabilities
- Finishing primary school and getting ready for high school

The teachers wanted to start with a discussion on bullying. Some important questions around this topic helped me decide on how this would be handled.

For example:

- What are the different forms of bullying?
- What are the underlying causes?
- How does bullying affect the child who is targeted?
- How do parents detect signs of their child being bullied?
- How do schools deal with bully tactics?

I went home to prepare my talk for the staff. The first staff development workshop was scheduled for next week. I could tell my hubby was interested in what I was doing and proud of my new appointment.

'So, what is your topic?' he asked.

I told him it was going to be about bullying. He raised his eyebrows. Then proceeded to tell me how rife bullying was in a boy's boarding school. Boys together, away from home, were often bullied. Standing up to the bully required a great deal of inner strength. I knew it had been hard at school for my husband, and his father had not helped the situation. Well, I would share my ideas with my husband, and I knew that he would be able to empathise with the topic.

I found this quote and felt it was a moving one:

'When people hurt you over and over, think of them like sandpaper. They may scratch and hurt you a bit, but in the end, you end up polished, and they end up useless.' Chris Colfer, an American actor and author.'

Yes, standing up to bullying was important, but for many children, it is beyond their abilities to stand up to a bully and his mates. I knew this was a critical topic and started to organise my talk for the teachers.

Workshop 1

Bullying: What it is, types of bullying, signs of bullying, and how to help

What it is and the kinds of bullying children may experience:

Bullying is all about using your power over someone else through physical, verbal, or social abuse. There is a wide range of bully tactics. All of them are hurtful and nasty. Teasing excessively, physically hurting someone, ignoring a child, or mentally making them feel belittled with hurtful comments. It can happen in schools, socially, in homes, and in offices. Bullies operate on the bus, via the phone, and in your neighbourhood; children even experience bullying in their own homes.

This form of unkind behaviour is very destructive to anyone who is being made the victim of a bully. It erodes self-esteem and confidence and can ruin a child's life. A bully delights in making someone feel bad about themselves, because generally, the bully does not feel good about themself. Bullying can involve an individual or a group who decides picking on others gives them a sense of power.

Signs of bullying to look out for:

There are several signs to look out for in children who may be the victims of some bullying at school or home.

Changes in eating patterns

Children at school may isolate themselves and not eat their lunch. They may push their food around the plate at home, showing complete disinterest in the delicious food for dinner.

Changes in sleep patterns

Look out for insomnia, demands for attention at bedtime, or the pitter-patter of tiny feet as a child cannot get to sleep. Dark rings under a child's eyes at school show a lack of sleep.

Emotional changes

Sudden tears or expressions are signs of emotional stress. Some children finally have to release their emotions, and a display of tears or anger for no apparent reason could be a sign of bullying.

Physical changes

Feeling ill in the morning before going to school or in class as the day begins is another sign that something is not correct. Children who are being bullied can feel terrible about being at school and have a tummy ache. They may feel physically ill at the thought of facing the day if they are being bullied.

Changes in communication

If you see something is wrong, but the child refuses to talk about the problem, there is something wrong at school. Children can just close up and will not discuss anything to do with how they are feeling.

Changes in their mood

Mood swings are a sure sign of being bullied. It is so traumatic the child may experience changes in their emotions and cannot handle the terrible feelings they have when they have to go to school.

Changes to their behaviour at home

Aggressive behaviour at home could be another indicator that something is wrong. The child experiencing bullying may become aggressive at home themselves as they try to deal with school bullying tactics.

Signs of depression

If you notice withdrawal symptoms as the child concerned may become depressed, that is a warning sign. The intense bullying may cause a child to stammer.

Physical signs of harmful behaviour

The child may have unexplained bruises, cuts, or scratches. They will make excuses about how they got these bruises.

Signs of damaged or missing belongings

Some bullies take vulnerable children's things. They will take their lunch or books, even items of clothing.

How can you help?

When you notice the signs of bullying or suspect there is bullying in the school or home; there are some steps to take. It is essential to listen and get the child who is being bullied into opening up and talking about what is happening. Try not to be emotional because your feelings may cloud your decisions and make you act irrationally.

There are two sides to this story. Parents who suspect bullying at school need to contact the school and determine what is happening through intervention with the teachers.

Teachers who suspect bullying at home need to contact the child's parents and meet with them.

Bullying is not acceptable in any circumstances, so you want to get to the bottom of the behaviour. It is crucial to find out what is happening and encourage children to share their feelings and act accordingly.

Mr Boardman and the staff were so appreciative of the discussion and creating an awareness of bullying in the school.

'Thank you, Mrs Lovemore. I think we have to share this message with our parents too,' said Mr Boardman. He initiated a parent evening to let me share this information with the parents.

My husband was equally proud of me, and then I knew the rest of the workshops and parent evenings I had planned would be easy to prepare.

The next topics on my list of staff suggestions were peer pressure, gang behaviour, and resolving conflict. Peer pressure is always a current topic. Close to bullying in many ways, but so often, children find they have to conform to others' ideas just to fit in.

Fashion trends, having the latest 'techno-gadgets, and following pop stars or movie heroes and heroines seem to be part of growing up. However, at what point does this behaviour cross over into the realms of undesirable influences?

Peer pressure can be a form of bullying. It seems more prevalent in teens and at the pre-teen stages of school life. Children susceptible to this form of influence may find peer pressure is something they cannot stand up to in adult life either. Teachers were worried about peer pressure in the school. Several parents had raised the issue too.

Workshop 2

Peer pressure: Gang behaviour and resolving conflict

What is peer pressure?

Peer pressure is the way other children influence children in their group. They are encouraged by pressure from the group to follow the same values and behaviours and conform to their attitudes and influences.

In my research into the subject, I came across a rather shocking statistic. Peer pressure can start in the middle-school years, as early as the pre-teen age. Children at this age are very conscious of making friendships and being with the right crowd. As they mature, the pressure from peers grows, and if they have not managed to learn to stand firm when pressured, they will become swayed into experimenting with alcohol and drugs and other risky behaviours. It was a genuine concern for parents and teachers.

There are six forms of peer pressure that I shared with the staff:

1. Spoken pressure
Children can be coerced into conforming to a group and their behaviours. It is easier for children to resist one child's pressure, but the group all pressing on a child to do something they know is wrong is far more challenging to resist.

2. Unspoken pressure

This is how young teens find themselves following fashion trends and music trends, pop idols and hair trends. Many of these teen trends are harmless and part of growing up while learning to make your own choices. One of the most well-worn phrases of this age is that everyone else has what children want or do what they want to do.

3. Direct pressure

Children who are not prepared for this kind of pressure may find themselves easily influenced by the pressure to accept an alcoholic drink or experiment with some daring activity, just to be accepted by the group. Direct pressure in a group situation is an exceedingly tricky scenario for any vulnerable teen to face.

4. Indirect pressure

In these situations, children may be influenced by what they see. They feel it is acceptable because they see other children involved in the activity. It may be through a movie or listening to gossip at school that makes them think the behaviour discussed is something they need to be involved in too.

5. Negative pressure

Being accepted by the crowd is essential to many young people. They want to be seen to be part of 'the crowd'. They want to follow the leaders of these groups. The easily influenced child will find it very difficult not to be in the crowd that is considered trendy, modern, daring, and just plain cool. The pressure of the wrong group results in negative influences and bad decisions.

6. Positive pressure

Not all pressure from groups of children is harmful. Picking the right crowd to follow will have a positive influence on the children in that crowd. Finding good wholesome role models and healthy relationships is especially important. This is the kind of group pressure you as a parent would favour. There are often great youth organisations and societies where children are encouraged to go on outings and camps and receive positive input and guidance in a like-minded group.

The staff could relate to these different forms of peer pressure, but how could the school help parents be better informed? The consensus was that a talk from a social worker, someone experienced with this age group, would be a good guest speaker at our next parent workshop.

Parents of children in this vulnerable age group were invited to a parent's evening just for them. The school organised a local social worker to address the parents on peer pressure and addictive behaviour. It was a tough evening for everyone, but parents were made aware of the genuine dangers their young teens could face.

The social worker spoke from real-life experiences of all kinds of addictions.

Food addictions, alcohol addiction, drug addiction, shopping addictions, gambling, gaming, and even sex addictions. It was a shocking list of different habits that could affect vulnerable children.

Fortunately, there were some unbelievably valuable pearls of wisdom shared too. Parents, myself included, could go home knowing some things could be done to support children during these difficult years leading up to adulthood.

The best support parents can give their children is a positive, nurturing home environment. Parents who are good role models and encourage healthy communication by discussing these topics with their children offer the best foundation for growing up able to face peer pressure.

Parents need to teach their children positive ways to deal with negative peer pressure. I remembered when I was growing up that there was peer pressure then. There was always someone doing things you wanted to do. One day, Mum was so fed up with me quoting what Angie, the spoilt only child of the class, could always do, she said to me:

'If Angie put her head in the fire, would you?' I was stunned at the comment.

It was brought on by frustration, but it was a wake-up call for me.

'No,' I remember saying. '*I would not be so silly!'*

My mum smiled, shrugged her shoulders, and walked away. She had made her point.

The social worker gave a few practical ideas of how parents could handle their teens and the transition from childhood to young adults:

• Be good role models and show your children how to have healthy friendships and enjoy family-orientated outings.

• Keep an open-door policy at home about discussing alcohol and drug-related issues. Always be truthful and answer questions as best you can.

• Encourage your children to think before making a decision. Come and discuss it with you if necessary. Talk about the consequences of their actions.

• When your children start going to gatherings with other young children, youth organisations or teen parties, be the parent that drops off your child and fetches them too. Or organise a lift club to be sure you know where your child is and how they are getting home.

She spoke about resolving conflict, and as I looked around the room, I saw parents nodding in agreement. The pre-teen and teen years seemed full of conflicting situations. The conflict was evident as hormones began to come into play, and signs of puberty and growing up was clear. Conflict was a particular hallmark of growing up.

What is the best way to help our children handle conflict?

It was a leading question. Here are five helpful suggestions:

1. Help children to get in touch with their feelings
At school and home, discussing feelings is a way to understand others and how they may feel in a conflict situation. Children who are in touch with their emotions can use empathy towards others and resolve conflict amicably. Ask questions like, 'How did you feel when...,' or 'How did someone else feel at that time?'

2. Encourage good listening skills

Being a good listener is an important life skill. It is shown by your own example of how to be a good listener. Encourage your child to listen to the other side of the argument and not to overreact.

3. **Take time to problem-solve together**

The opportunity to talk through different problem scenarios opens communication lines within the family and helps children learn about conflict resolution. Families can use the dinner table talk to encourage discussions on conflict resolution.

4. **Help children learn from their mistakes**

Parents can help children look objectively at their mistakes and learn how to do things better to develop a positive solution. It may not be the one a child is hoping for, but helping children to see that making mistakes is part of learning to grow up is important too.

5. **Get help in difficult situations**

Teach your children as they grow up that they can always count on you for advice and wisdom. Encourage the kind of relationship that allows for good communication skills between parents, teachers, and children.

I was so grateful to be part of a school that guided parents and teachers interested in the children's best outcomes. It was not just about academics. The school was there with parental support, and the teachers were approachable and friendly. It was such a pleasure to be involved as a parent and a member of staff.

Kerry was in her last year at primary school. She had one more year to get through, and we were looking for a suitable high school for her. The school had arranged visits to different high schools for the children, and there was plenty of excitement building up in her class for the next stage of education.

Nikki was starting her middle-school grades but was not doing so well. She had compensated in many ways for not reading and writing confidently, but she fell behind as the workload became more intense. There was a problem, but we did not understand precisely what it was.

Tears in the morning and a reluctance to read, although she loved stories and books, indicated an underlying problem. She did not like school, and she hated homework. What was I going to do with my Nikki?

I made an appointment with her class teacher, and my husband and I went together to present a united front. I knew there was a problem in the classroom because the third-grade teacher had Nikki right in front of the class. The school had a protocol to follow if parents were concerned about their child:

- An interview with the teacher.
- An assessment with a specialist if necessary.
- Working together as a team—school, parents, and remedial specialist.
- Explaining the process and the problems to the child.
- Keeping lines of communication open.

It was a very encouraging interview, and I realised there was a need to address the policy of 'how to recognise difficulties in class early on.' Did Nikki have a learning difficulty or perhaps a disability? I needed to recognise the difference between 'difficulty' and 'disability'. I decided to research the topic for my own benefit and as part of a workshop for the library teachers.

Workshop 3

Academic difficulties: How to recognise difficulties and address them early on

First, we need to address the difference between a difficulty and a disability.

Learning difficulties:

In simple terms, a learning difficulty affects the way you learn. The brain cannot process, analyse, receive, or store information. There are several learning difficulties.

Dyslexia, dyscalculia, and dyspraxia are some of the 'dysfunctions' that can be encountered early on in a child's school career.

Learning disabilities:

Learning disabilities affect the way children learn and how they perform in society. A disability influences all walks of life and especially learning at school.

The autism spectrum, Down syndrome, and spina bifida can all cause learning disabilities. Specialist intervention is crucial and early diagnosis from a SENCo, a Special Needs Educational Coordinator, is vital.

Other academic difficulties may include mental health issues, attention deficit disorder, anxiety, and visual or auditory problems. Early intervention is the best possible route to finding solutions.

Here are some signs to look for as teachers and parents.

- Difficulty learning to read and write.
- Struggling with maths and number work.
- Difficulty paying attention.
- Having a poor memory.
- Disorganised and clumsy.

The most common difficulties fall into three categories: dyslexia, dyscalculia, and dysgraphia.

Dyslexia is associated with language skills, like reading, writing, spelling, and using words. Children with dyslexia have problems connecting letters and sounds. They may even have difficulty expressing themselves verbally.

Dyscalculia is associated with an inability to work with numbers. Learning to count and calculate simple sums would be an indicator of some level of dyscalculia. Memorising times tables would be complex for a child with dyscalculia.

Dysgraphia is associated with handwriting abilities and putting ideas down on paper.

Other processing disorders affect auditory and visual processing and attention or concentration. It is through early intervention that problems can be detected. Solutions are found through remediation and intervention from a paediatrician or the help of a remedial specialist.

Specialists focused on child-related learning problems include paediatricians, clinical psychologists, and developmental psychologists like me. All are trained to look out for the symptoms shown by children as they struggle with school progress. There are occupational therapists, speech therapists, language therapists, and programmes to help children with learning difficulties. The school, class teacher, and parents working together can do wonders for children with learning difficulties.

After the workshop, the teachers were grateful for the relevant information, and the school drew up a process of intervention with names of doctors and specialists to refer to. It was reassuring for parents to know the school was proactive. Nikki was assessed and started remedial lessons to improve auditory and visual processing. It is always difficult for parents to find they have a child who is struggling for any reason. Facing this reality with my background did not make it any easier, but it helped me empathise with other parents in this situation.

Two little girls from the same parents, in the same school, but quite different in personality, academic focus, and performance. How important it was for parents to accept each child with their differences. We are the ones to guide and nurture the children we bring into this world.

I was reminded of an extract I read from one of my favourite verses from the chapter on children written by Kahlil Gibran in *The Prophet*.

'You are the bows from which your children

As living arrows are sent forth.

The archer sees the mark upon the path of the infinite,

And He bends you with His might

That His arrows may go swift and far.

Let your bending in the archer's hands be for gladness;

For even as He loves the arrow that flies,

So He loves also the bow that is stable.'

We felt stable and content with our little family, but life has a way of dealing different cards sometimes. I discovered in Kerry's last year at primary school that I was pregnant with our third child. Once I had recovered from the shock, there were exciting things to plan and new beginnings for all of us.

CHAPTER SEVEN

ESSENTIAL LIFE LESSONS TO IMPART ON YOUR LITTLE ONES

S ometimes a surprise comes along in our lives, and at first, we are totally shocked. I know I was not expecting to have a third child. At first, the whole idea did not fit well with my own plans. I was settled at the school and enjoyed being part of the system. Schools are like little mini societies, and once you are there, you feel like family. The girls were settled, and Kerry was doing well. She would be going to high school next year. Nikki continued to have a kind of love-hate relationship with the school. She loved her friends and was very pleasant, but somehow the teachers never understood our Nikki. I always knew at parenting interviews we would find Nikki had been put at the front of the class, where the teacher could keep a watchful eye on my daughter.

Now, despite thinking I had everything under control, I discovered my life was about to change. Ashley Montagu, a well-known anthropologist, said this about surprises.

'The moments of happiness we enjoy take us by surprise.

It's not that we seize them, but that they seize us.'

His words made me reflect on this new surprise. Once I had come to terms with being pregnant, I could take in moments of happiness with the surprise. The idea of adding to our family had seized all of us. My husband and I decided to tell the girls when we knew if the new addition would be a boy or a girl. When my husband found out the new baby would be a boy, he was ecstatic —another man in the family. I smiled, well yes, I thought, but there was some growing up to do to get to that stage.

Telling the girls brought about mixed emotions. Kerry was extremely excited and asked all sorts of questions about the baby. When would he arrive and what would his name be and could she bath him and take him for walks and, and, and...?

Nikki did not look as if she liked the idea of a baby in the family at all. Her nose was put out of joint, and I could see some future sibling rivalry incidents appearing on the scene. It was something I expected because our two little girls have pretty different personalities. I made a note to myself to make sure Nikki was included in the new arrival's routine. This would be an opportunity to teach some character-building life skills and positive growth for our little family.

I made a list of the top ten life skills to learn before turning ten years old. Ten out of ten would be a great score! I studied the list and chose three to work on with the girls as the new baby's time grew closer. I would not ignore the rest, but these three seemed most relevant to the coping skills needed for the arrival of a new baby.

The life skills were character-building too.

I chose:

- Be grateful—Have an attitude of gratitude.

- Do not be envious—Envy makes you feel miserable inside.

- Needs and wants—Learn the difference between our needs and wants.

How do you teach children under the age of ten to be grateful?

It starts with appreciating little things. Mother Nature abounds with beautiful things to be grateful for. I enjoyed taking the girls out for nature walks when they were little and noticing all kinds of exciting and beautiful things along the way. Kerry loved flowers and different wild grasses. Nikki was more interested in creepy crawlies, but as a family, we could enjoy a nature walk and talk about how grateful we were for the little things around us.

Helping one another brings about an attitude of gratitude. Getting everyone involved in a few chores around the house with a big thank you from me or their dad showed how adults accept acts of kindness with gratitude. The new baby was growing as my pregnancy carried over the next few months. Kerry loved feeling the baby move. She expressed her appreciation for the new brother she was looking forward to meeting. Nikki huffed and puffed her way out into the garden, where I could see her sitting on a bench muttering to herself. She was not in the gratitude category.

Learning gratitude keywords like 'please' and 'thank you' helps children to feel grateful. My Mum called them P's and Q's. I shared Mum's phrase, 'mind your P's and Q's', at the dinner table once. The children did not understand what I meant at first and made funny faces. They liked peas, they said, but cucumber was not nice at all. When I explained that P's and Q's were please and thank you, everyone laughed, and the message stuck forever. The message of gratitude.

THE SECOND CHARACTER TRAIT I WANTED THE GIRLS TO LEARN WAS NOT BEING ENVIOUS

I knew Nikki was going to envy the fuss made of the new baby. She was about to be toppled off her 'youngest kid in the family' block. She would be envious of the extra time spent with the baby, and I could see she was already jealous of the interest everyone was showing in the anticipated new arrival. Kerry was so excited, and that made things worse.

Envy or jealousy is an emotion that has been around for centuries.

Aristotle, the Greek philosopher, said:

> *'Envy is pain at the good fortune of others.'*

That spelled out the feeling of envy in a nutshell. Nikki felt pain about the new arrival, not the joy and excitement that her older sister experienced. The way to explain envy and get the feelings out into the open was to talk about different kinds of envy or jealousy. What could I relate to in terms of the causes of jealousy, and would sharing these ideas with the girls help Nikki, in particular, to overcome her feelings of jealousy? Perhaps Kerry had some envious moments about other things. In reality, we all have feelings of envy at some stage of our lives, and it is how we deal with these emotions that lead to positive outcomes.

What are the common causes of envy?

- Envy of material things
- Envy of academics or skills
- Social envy
- Sibling envy

Envy of material things:

Children are more likely to envy material things when they get to primary school and compare what they have with other children's items. It may start with simple things like pencil crayons or some fancy sports kit. After a while, children begin to visit or go to parties at other homes and see different games and technical things they may covet. It is a trap that children may fall into, and something parents need to stop before it begins to make children miserable. This is where gratitude plays a part in steering children away from envy; they stop negative feelings about other children's things.

Mealtimes are great times to connect with the family and share things everyone is grateful for. Parents can be vulnerable at this time and share stories from their childhood linked to envy. My husband and I decided to tell the girls what we envied as children.

My husband told the girls about his childhood on the farm. His family was not wealthy. They had close friends who lived on a mine. The gold miners were well off, but the farmers were always struggling. My husband said he desperately wanted a motorbike. A real one like his mining friend had. When he visited his friend at the mine, he rode his friend's motorbike around on the safe mine roads. It had big shiny rear-view mirrors and made motorbike noises. The boys on the farm had pedal bikes. They clipped cardboard onto the fork of the bicycle under the brakes. When they rode the bikes, the cardboard made a motorbike noise. It was the sound of the card as it was flipped by the spokes on the wheel. They found a way to tape hand mirrors onto the bikes, and away they rode around the farm.

My husband laughed as he remembered the fun he had on his farm bike. The girls laughed, too, especially as their father made bizarre motorbike noises.

Then it was my turn. I remembered living in a quiet neighbourhood in a small but comfortable house. On the other side of the road were more extensive, more flashy houses. Directly opposite us lived an only child who had everything. She had the most incredible doll's house, a beautifully decorated bedroom, and a 'Betsy Wetsy' doll. Oh my, I told the girls, this doll could really wet its diaper, and if you pushed its tummy, it cried real tears. I really wanted a 'Betsy Wetsy' doll and all the other lovely things an only child had because she was very spoilt. Then I remembered going to visit one day and my friend, who had everything, was crying.

Kerry and Nikki's eyes were wide open with anticipation for the reason why the girl who had everything was crying. I paused for a moment so the girls could think about this sad turn of events.

'Why was she crying?' asked Kerry.

Then I explained she was sad because she was lonely, and an only child sometimes wishes she had a brother or a sister. Kerry smiled and said how lucky she felt because she was going to have a baby brother. Nikki totally missed the point and asked if her dad could put a motorbike card on her little bicycle.

It was not going to be easy for Nikki to accept another sibling.

Sibling envy was going to be a hot topic in our family. I know it is normal behaviour among brothers and sisters. There had not been much rivalry between our girls. They were pretty different, and a nearly four-year age gap meant they were not rivals at school. When Kerry started school, Nikki was still at playschool, and when Nikki began school, Kerry was on her way to the more senior classes. Now when Nikki gets to the senior end of the school system, Kerry will be moving on into high school. I shuddered for a moment. My eldest daughter was rapidly approaching her teen years.

My husband and I were very aware of handling each child differently. I was grateful we were having a boy next because another girl would have been harder for Nikki to accept. She was probably feeling very uncertain about precisely what a new baby would mean and would she have to give up everything to make way for this little being.

We decided not to make an issue of the new arrival and how the girls would feel. I thought too much discussion on the new baby might make things worse in Nikki's mind. We sat out in the garden a few weeks before the baby was due and talked about NEEDS and WANTS. It was an exciting conversation. Kerry's maturity shone through as she understood how our bodies need food and water, and we need love and safety. She had the maturity to understand our needs are different at different ages. We talked about what the baby would need and how we would want to help the baby.

Nikki stood up, folded her arms. She glared at Kerry and me and said in a loud voice!

'I do not NEED or WANT a baby brother!'

Then she stormed off to the garage, leaving us all speechless. My husband came to the rescue and went to finish the motorbike sound effects for Nikki's bicycle. She was immensely proud of her bike. It was her first two-wheeler, and although she still needed training wheels, she was delighted to have a bicycle instead of a tricycle.

Envy and the middle-child syndrome.

I could see we were heading for some envy and inevitable jealousy from the family's middle child. Nikki was going to feel very jealous of the new baby. Added to that, as Kerry grew older and had some considerable sister privileges, I could see Nikki feeling hard done by because she was not in the same position. She would be the middle child, and we would have to deal with the emotional outbursts and sibling jealousy. I found some valuable advice to help take the pressure off sibling rivalry and the obvious envy from Nikki. I was sure this form of envy must affect other families. It probably filters through to adult life if it is not sorted out while the children are young.

These five suggestions were most helpful:

1. Do not highlight jealous feelings.

It is essential to focus on helping with feelings and show children ways to deal with how they feel in the situation they find themselves in. Diffuse the anger or envy by acknowledging that it is there. It is normal to feel envious of the time and attention given to one child, mainly if it is a baby. Babies need extra attention while they are very small. I read that it is an excellent idea to unfocus on the sibling, or the baby, causing envy and, instead, focus on the jealous child. Simply boost the ego of the jealous child by finding good things that child can do. Try to make a jealous child feel helpful and wanted. Praising the jealous child for little positive things and giving them ways to feel good about themselves boost their confidence and self-esteem.

2. Make some special one-on-one time for the other sibling.

Making a conscious effort to spend quality time with each of the children reduces the jealous feelings between siblings. It takes some planning, but individual time with a jealous sibling may be all that it takes to change their perception of how you feel about them. Set aside time to read a book or do a puzzle or bake cookies together. Find something to do that the baby or other siblings cannot do at that time. Have a happy conversation during the time you are together. During this quality time, be sure to encourage self-esteem as you tell your jealous child how great they are and how wonderful it is to spend time with them.

3. **Do not lay blame at the feet of either sibling.**

As children grow up, it is normal to have altercations. Try not to blame one child over the other. Recognise rivalry is bound to take place, and you may never know who really started an incident. When the children are older, do not blame one child over the other. Acknowledge the disagreement and find something else to do with each child. Often it is a fickle argument, and just a change of scene or a different game will sort out the jealous feelings.

4. **Find a neutral zone.**

This is where you put on your neutral parent hat. Discuss the facts of the situation. Acknowledge the feelings without judgement. You do not have to agree with your child or take sides during the argument or demonstration of rivalry. You agree with what your child is thinking and feeling. Being a good listener is helpful and may just be enough to change the perception in some situations.

5. **Suggest a solution.**

Part of your role in parenting siblings who envy each other in finding and suggesting a solution. Sometimes it is all that is needed, a diversion from the aggravating factor. If there is no acceptable solution to the cause of envy at the time, then perhaps the problem just boils down to some more time with mum. Let your child know they have your attention and spend some 'Mummy and me time' with each child.

Then one day, we ran into an actual argument that was just not resolving itself. I could see Nikki was tired, and Kerry had now run out of patience with her younger sister. Nikki and Kerry had been arguing that afternoon about who should pack away a game they had been playing. The house rules are that the winner packs up. It is a way of being more humble over your win. In this instance, they had stopped the game earlier, so there was no clear winner or loser because they quit playing the game. Nikki had decided she did not want to play any longer. Kerry had been very patient with her, but now an argument arose over who would pack up the game. It was clear there was no resolution to the dispute. I intervened, and the three of us packed away the game together.

That evening, at supper time, I decided to get some input from the girl's father. I asked him how arguments were solved in his family. He had a twinkle in his eyes when he answered.

> *'My dad would go to the games cupboard in the hallway and get out the boxing gloves. He would hand each of the brothers who were arguing a pair of boxing gloves and say:*
>
> *' "Go on, boys, sort yourselves out and stop arguing over nothing. May the best man win!" '*

Nikki stared wide-eyed at her dad, and Kerry had a nervous giggle.

> *'Really,'* I said. Then I added, *'Do we have boxing gloves?'*

At that moment, the girls decided it was a silly argument and boxing was not the solution, but I could see Nikki was curious about the boxing story. She wanted to know who won these boxing matches.

'Who was the champion?' asked Nikki.

'Well,' said their dad. 'I was a flyweight champion, so I could out move my brother. We never got to punch each other because I dodged out of the way, and he kept missing me. Finally, we ended up laughing so much we stopped the fight and forgot what we were really fighting about!'

Well, that set the girls off laughing at the idea of their dad being a flyweight, and when he explained there were featherweights and bantamweights too, they laughed even more. It was good to all laugh together, as they say, laughter is the best medicine, and it can heal disputes too!

After supper, we agreed boxing gloves and girls were never going to resolve rivalry or envy. What could we do as a family to resolve disputes?

A peaceful solution, but a wise one too.

When the girls had gone to bed, still giggling about their dad being a flyweight, my husband and I sat down to discuss how we could handle disputes in future.

'I remember this from my boxing days,' said my husband very seriously. *It was Sugar Ray Leonard, thought to be the greatest boxer of all time, who said*

this:

'Every move you make starts with your heart, and that's in rhythm, or you are in trouble.'

Our solution needed to come from the heart. We decided then that we would apply empathy and teach the girls to be in touch with their feelings. This process would be part of a 'time in' sharing of feelings. 'Time in' with one of their parents and 'time in' to come up with solutions. It would be a great way to build unity in our family. During the 'time in', they could bring different feelings to the surface and learn to understand them better. A 'time in' rather than a 'time out' to solve family altercations.

The next time we were together, my husband explained the 'time in' idea to the girls. He explained that partners would have time in the ring to spar with each other as a boxer in a true fighting fashion.

'When you are sparring, you are practising your moves, and the boxers always bump fists to start. It is a sign of respect before the game.' The girls were so taken with this idea; it became our family tradition of beginning a 'time in' discussion.

Having a sense of family is another way to resolve differences and help one another to give support and empathy. That day I felt as if I had been a bit like Sugar Ray Leonard, and making moves with my heart was definitely the way to go.

The days were racing by, and my time at the school was ending. The teachers organised a baby shower with beautiful clothes for boys. When I took the gifts home, I got the expected excitement from Kerry. She was happily putting the little, blue baby grows and toys for boys away in the nursery. We had turned the large walk-in dressing room into a neat little nursery off the main bedroom. The nursery theme was cars–very boyish—and when we put up some of the posters of Lightning McQueen, I saw Nikki's face light up just for a moment. I felt hopeful about a connection between the middle child with her tomboy nature and the new addition to the family.

That evening, at bedtime, I read a story to Nikki about welcoming a new baby. I think she appreciated the time we spent together, just the two of us, and the reassurance that the baby was never going to take her place. There was a glimmer of hope as we spoke about the boyish things Nikki loved. The cars and the karate classes and the fun in the mud activities boys love so much. I could feel her coming round to the idea of a baby brother, but it would be difficult to tell until the new baby arrived. I chose a Joanna Cole book to read to Nikki.

The Joanna Cole books were perfect, and her *Magic School Bus* stories were favourites in the library. The book about a new baby in the house had such beautiful illustrations. Real photographs, and both the girls loved the book. The other Joanna Cole book I enjoyed was called 'I Am a Big Sister'. I hoped Nikki would start to feel really important with her new title of 'Big Sister'.

Thank goodness for the library, I thought. A wealth of lovely books and, for me, a place I had enjoyed working in for the last few years. It was now time to give a final workshop for the children in the senior primary and the parents. The plan was to invite parents, and after the workshop, have a little farewell gathering for me. Not goodbye, I assured everyone because I had Kerry and Nikki at the school and a future pupil in a few years to come.

I decided an equipping class for the children about basic healthy life skills would be a good idea. Then something similar for the parents to help them prepare their children for life outside of school. No academics here, simply good habits and life skills.

First up was something for the children. I made a shortlist of six habits, or secrets of success, to encourage healthy daily living. A summary of the workshop for the children was made to send home to the parents.

CHILDREN'S WORKSHOP/ SUMMARY FOR THE PARENTS:

SIX SECRETS OF SUCCESS FOR DAILY LIVING.

1. Eat right: Healthy eating habits

Healthy eating habits are not just about the food you eat. First and foremost, parents need to be good role models. Teach portion control to your children and help them avoid too many sweets and processed food. A healthy diet with fruit and vegetables is to be encouraged. Try to eat the main meal of the day at the table as a family. Teach your children about different food groups and vitamins and the right food to eat a balanced diet. Helping children be aware of what they are eating and how it benefits them to grow healthy and strong is a good life skill.

2. Sleep right: The importance of getting enough sleep

The bedtime routine is an essential part of the daily schedule. Most parenting books on this topic will advise that a bedtime routine is the best way to instil an excellent attitude to sleep. The bedtime routine starts a while before actually getting into bed. A good bedtime routine takes care of teeth brushing and a wind-down time with a bedtime story. If your child is potty or toilet trained, the last action before lights out should be a visit to the bathroom. Then it's good night prayers or saying some things you are grateful for that day to end off the routine in a positive, relaxed way. Tailor your routine to suit the age of your child and their needs. The younger children will need an earlier routine and a very consistent one. Older children may need some time to go over their homework with you and share some school-related problems. Ensure your child is ready to go to sleep, feeling relaxed and safe in their sleep environment. Little ones may need a cuddly toy or a soothing blanket for comfort.

3. **Fresh air and outdoor play: Keep active**

Physical health, social integration, and breathing good clean air are the benefits of getting outdoors. Running, jumping, climbing, throwing, kicking balls, and playing outdoor games build children's motor skills. Outdoor play builds confidence and social relationships. It encourages children to learn about balance and safety as they play at different levels. Playing outdoors helps children feel in touch with the real world.

4. **Safety rules: Warning signs about danger, and stranger danger too**

Here is a quick checklist of the most important.

• Know your name and a contact number. Physical safety and personal safety are high on the list of safety rules to teach all children. Children should know their names and surname. They should also know their physical address and a phone number to contact when they are old enough.

• Stranger danger. Teach children not to talk to strangers or accept anything from strangers like sweets or anything to drink.

• Do not go out into the street alone. Teach children they must be accompanied by an adult. Mum or Dad should be there to allow them out of the gate. They should not climb the fence or the gate because they are there for their safety.

• Playing with fire is strictly forbidden. No matches or lighters or fireworks or gas cookers to be lit, ever.

• Keep your body private. Do not allow others to touch you in places that are intimate parts of your body.

• If you get lost, stay where you are and look for another mother with children or a person in a uniform who could help you. Remember to only share your address with someone who looks reliable. Explain to your children about security personnel or police officers who can help. It is essential not to wander away, but rather stay close to where you got lost so your mum will find you.

• Show your child early on about plugs and hair dryers, and electrical equipment they should not use.

• Make sure medicines and medicine cabinets are out of reach.

5. **Hygiene: Keeping clean**

Here are essential habits for every family.

• Hand washing:

Washing hands with soap and water is probably at the top of the list of healthy habits. Little people have their hands in all kinds of interesting, but not so clean, spaces all day. Teaching the washing of hands habit is an excellent way of protecting children from germs. The most crucial hand wash time is before meals and after using the toilet.

- <u>Oral hygiene</u>:

Children need to learn how to look after their teeth and have good oral hygiene habits. Start a healthy routine of brushing twice a day. In the morning after breakfast and in the evening before bedtime. Little ones can get used to a toothbrush with parents' supervision early on in their bedtime routine. As the second set of teeth come in, the brushing and introduction of flossing become necessary. Gargling and brushing gums and even the tongue all helps to keep the mouth clean. Teach your child to avoid sweets and cool drinks loaded with sugar.

- <u>Hair and nail hygiene</u>:

A good scrub with a nail brush helps to keep dirt from collecting under fingernails. Keep a nail brush in the bathroom and use it at bath time. Show children how to clip their nails and help with this while they are too young to handle clippers or nail scissors. Good hair care helps with keeping the scalp clean and hair looking healthy. Regular washing, at least twice a week and brushing every day, maintains healthy hair and scalp. Children will need help with hair washing, especially if their hair is long.

- <u>Home hygiene</u>:

Help children to take care of their personal space at home. Keep them interested in helping around the house with chores and cleaning up if they make a mess. Keeping the bathroom and toilet area clean and tidy is especially important.

6. **Out and about: Public behaviour**

Going out with young children can be hazardous unless you are confident that they will behave. Have your family safety rules in place. Don't allow your little one to run around the restaurant unless it is one of those 'kid friendly' restaurants that gives children the right to run around. Teach your children to speak politely to the waitress and be aware of other families in the restaurant. Eating out teaches good life skills of consideration and exemplary behaviour. Do not allow your child to go to the public bathrooms without an adult. Make sure they practise their healthy hand washing. Teach good manners at the table and how to order politely.

After the children's workshop, I gave copies of the notes for all the children to take home to their parents. It was an excellent way to pass on the information.

That evening, because I had been so busy with workshops and finalising my last few days at school, I felt pretty tired. My husband suggested we go out as a family to a restaurant. What a good idea, I thought. I was a bit concerned about Nikki because she was not used to dining out. Then I remembered it was one of the secrets of success. Going out and about and being considerate. It was time to practise what I preached. When we arrived at the restaurant, we met some friends at the door with their toddler, James. We decided to sit together and have some family time with them. Kerry and Nikki were excited to see friends, and the restaurant was reasonably 'kid-friendly'. There was face painting for the children and a games room. Then my dear friend Wendy began to tell me about the eating problems she was having with James.

> *'He will only eat if we make aeroplane noises as I wave the spoon of food out in front of him. He rides around the table on his tricycle and stops in every so*

often for a mouthful of food that I have to feed him,'
she said.

I could see Wendy was quite traumatised by the idea of being in a restaurant with her son and concerned about what would he do during supper time. They had arrived with James in a stroller. I looked around and realised there was no sign of James, Nikki, or the stroller. Then I heard the aeroplane noises, and from the corner of my eye, I saw Nikki pushing the stroller up the aisle to the table. I held my breath. What happened next was amazing.

Nikki knelt in front of the stroller and said to little James,

> *'We are at the airport; the plane has landed, and you have to get off now. Unfasten your seat belt and go and eat your supper with the rest of the crew!'*

James got out of the stroller, walked up to his mother, and sat down very politely for his supper. I could see Wendy was in shock. I cautioned her to just join in the game with Nikki and let James eat his supper with the rest of us.

Wendy phoned me after the meal and thanked me for helping her find a way to stop this terrible table behaviour and the drama she had to get James to eat.

I laughed and gave the credit to Nikki.

In my final week at the school, I held a workshop for the mums and dads. It was quite an emotional evening, but once again, I felt I had been able to make a difference. This workshop was more about coping with basic life skills for older children and a way of showing senior children that one day they would have to manage on their own. Did they have some basic cooking skills? Could they shop at the supermarket? Would they know how to budget? Or a simple thing like wrapping a present and making a unique greeting card. I asked these questions to the group when they had settled down for the workshop.

The question was given to the parents. Did they think their children could do all twelve of the skills on the list? The shocking truth was that very few answered yes to all the items on the list of twelve basic life skills to prepare for the real world. It was also a sad fact that parents with boys in the family admitted the boys were less able to complete the list than the girls. Except for hammering a nail, the girls seemed to be savvier with essential life skills.

PARENTS' WORKSHOP:

12 Skills to Teach Your Children for the Real World

1. **Basic cooking:**

Encourage your children to learn some basic cooking skills. How to cook some vegetables, rice, and pasta. How to boil or scramble an egg. How to make soup or cottage pie. Just some straightforward meals, including breakfasts and making a packed lunch.

2. **Kitchen safety:**

Make sure children can use a knife without cutting themselves and a peeler. Teach them how to microwave or boil something on the stove. Washing up and keeping the kitchen tidy were included in kitchen safety.

3. **Doing the laundry:**

Equip your children with the knowledge and experience to load and switch on a washing machine. Make sure they know the different cycles and how to hang their clothes. Show older children the basic skills required to use an iron and to recognise not all our clothes need ironing if they are hung and folded correctly.

4. **Giving and following directions:**

Start early on with little games involving turning right or left and take steps in this direction or that direction. Get to know your neighbourhood. Learn how to direct people how to get to your house from the school or supermarket.

5. **Basic chores around the house:**

Know how to sweep and dust. Children should know how to keep their room tidy and make their own beds, put away laundry, and wash the car. All of these skills are useful to know for running a household or student home someday.

6. **Shopping at the supermarket:**

Go on a shopping expedition together and show your child how to be selective and look for the best prices. Teach them how to weigh items and choose vegetables or fruit. Master the art of paying at the till.

7. **Simple first aid:**

Have a simple first aid kit, explain what is in it, and how to use the items if there is a need. Minor cuts and scratches can be treated at home. Keep the first aid box out of the reach of small children.

8. **Giving and receiving gifts.**

Teach your children how to wrap a special gift for someone who will appreciate it. Gift-giving is one of the pleasurable things we can all enjoy. Learn how to make a card and write a thank-you note.

9. **Hammering a nail:**

This may seem like a simple task, but how many children learn the hard way? Using tools and a hammer and nail requires coordination to avoid hammering your finger or thumb. Some basic safety rules for using tools and putting batteries in a torch or changing a light bulb would be helpful.

10. **Managing time:**

Being able to manage time effectively is an essential life skill. Start by giving your child an alarm clock to be aware of getting up on time. Then manage other time slots during the day. A weekly planner helps put aside time for everything during the week and keep after-school times for sport or homework. This creates an awareness of time.

11. **Managing money:**

Teach your children early on about money. Pocket money and tiny allowances introduce them to handling money. Help them to have goals they may be saving towards. Teach them about budgets and using their money wisely. Help them understand material differences among families. Introduce your child to a bank card and the safety factors of internet banking. These are all age-appropriate steps in understanding money.

12. **Standing up for yourself:**

Children can learn basic self-defence or be aware of what to do if they are in a dangerous situation. They should know who to call or how to get the proper attention. What <u>not</u> to do if a stranger approaches them is essential too. They should never accept lifts from people they don't know or anything a stranger may tempt them with.

A round of applause! And a word of thanks from the headmaster ended the evening. I expressed my gratitude for being part of the school and, in particular, the library. Many parents stayed for the snacks afterwards and came to thank me personally.

'What are you going to do?' they asked.

There were many questions to answer, but I knew that first and foremost, I was going to be back in the early mothering role again. This time I would be nurturing a boy, a son. I loved this quote; although the author is unknown, the words ring true.

> *'Son, you will outgrow my lap, but never my heart.'*

The little surprise was really filling me with such emotional joy. I thought of so many things I wanted to do, but my dear husband had said he thought I should just be a mum.

He reminded me of how much I loved writing.

> *'Why not start writing something small for mums. You have so much advice to give, and now could be the time to share your knowledge through writing,'* he said.

Our baby boy was due the following week. There was time to spend with the girls before they went to my mum. The gynaecologist had decided this should be a caesarean. Planned date, and I knew the girls would be happy with my mum for a couple of nights.

Kerry had the baby's crib already with soft toys, and she arranged and rearranged the blankets several times. She was extremely excited. Nikki was studying the *Car*'s pictures, and I could sense there was very little maternal empathy coming from her direction. We had finally made up our minds about the boy's name.

We chose two family names, Peter and John, and put them together to make Peter John. Peter or Potato Pete, the original farmer in the family. John, my husband's name, although he did not follow the farming tradition. The new addition to the

Lovemore family would be Peter John or PJ for short. Kerry loved the name, but she was so over the moon about the baby she liked everything connected to her new brother. Nikki was not impressed.

> *'PJ,'* she muttered. *'I am going to call him PJ, Pyjama Boy! That's what he will be, a baby in pyjamas. No fun in that!'*

That was a moment of truth! I realized then Nikki just thought the baby would be a baby, and that was that. In her mind, he was never going to grow up and be anything more than a pyjama boy.

We had a way to go with our Nikki. Hopefully, as the baby grew, she would find he was not a permanent baby—an exciting new phase for our family. A near-to teenage daughter and a baby boy, then caught in the middle, our angry bird, Nikki.

CHAPTER EIGHT

TRANSFORMATION - A PARENTS WORST NIGHTMARE

P eter John, PJ, aka Pyjama Boy, arrived, and we were overwhelmed with delight and welcome messages from family and friends. I loved this rhyme on one of the many cards we received:

'Little hands and little feet,

Little toothless grins so sweet.

Little eyes that shine so bright,

Little arms to hug you tight.

Everything is little, except your joy,

When you have a new baby boy.'

Aaah, everyone was delighted. Well, almost everyone. PJ's middle sister was not so happy. She just muttered about the pyjamas again, and it did seem as if PJ was only in pyjamas most of the time! He was wrapped in his baby grow and snuggled into his crib. A winter baby needed to be kept warm.

'What happened to snakes and snails and puppy dog tails?' asked Nikki one day.

I could tell Nikki just thought PJ was not unique in any way. What could he do that was any different from babies or dolls, for that matter? Then one day, Nikki came to watch me change PJ. Kerry was in the bathroom, getting the bath ready with bath toys, and I was busy getting the baby ready for his bath. Nikki, the innocent bystander, suddenly let out a yell of surprise. Just as I had taken off the baby's diaper, he decided that would be an excellent time to shoot at the moon with a stream of urine.

I thought Nikki would be furious! Well, to my surprise, this act of producing a fountain that went over her head and into the room totally impressed Nikki. She called her dad to see what had happened. Dad grinned from ear to ear at his son's prowess, and I shook my head. I guess boys will be boys, I thought.

After that, Nikki was more interested in her baby brother and what else he could do as he grew up. I was happy to see a bond developing between them. Kerry continued to play a significant sister role. She was accommodating, but as the year came to an end and high school was just around the corner, she had less time to be involved with a growing baby. She needed more time to prepare for the next phase of her schooling.

The school sent out information about high school and what we as parents could do to help our primary school leavers with the process of going to high school.

PREPARING FOR HIGH SCHOOL.

THERE WERE TEN TIPS FROM THE SCHOOL

1. Visit the high schools to get an idea of what to expect.

Children need to see and get a feel for the new environment. A school visit demystifies the transition from primary school into high school.

2. Encourage good study habits.

If studying has been a weak aspect of primary school, help your child to be more diligent in this area. Try to create routine study times at home as part of the homework sessions.

3. Help your child with time management.

Time management with schedules and pacing yourself to do tasks at a particular time are essential aspects of high school.

4. Make sure you have the right supplies for the first year at high school.

Get hold of the stationery list and uniform list to be sure your child has everything. Children just starting at high school do not want to stick out; they want to fit in.

5. Attend any orientation functions or information on the school opportunities.

Be sure to get hold of any information relevant to the first year. Join the class groups and assure your child you are there for support all the way.

6. Find out what extracurricular activities are offered.

Knowing what choices there are to suit your child's particular interests is essential. Be prepared with the right gear and help your child decide what to join for the activities.

7. Make sure you have the correct uniform.

Getting the proper uniform and having everything ready in time helps relieve any stress your child may feel about starting high school.

8. Get in touch with your child's feelings.

Build good communication skills between you and your child. You want them to come to you and discuss whatever is worrying them at high school.

9. Know how your child is getting to and from school.

This may seem trivial, but your child needs to know how they will get to their new school and what route to take. Where will they get out of the car, and how will they get to their classroom.

10. **Have some goals in place for year one at high school.**

Having some simple goals in place adds to feelings of security and a sense of purpose for your child as they start high school. Discuss these with your child, but keep them relevant and straightforward. Focus on the first year, not the final year and university.

We had to recognise our eldest daughter was about to enter an incredibly challenging phase of her life. Becoming a teenager, going to high school, and becoming more independent. New boundaries would have to be put in place for our growing teen and acceptance of some rocky road emotions as her hormones kicked in. Added to that, the force of peer pressure would be far more significant at high school. Toddlers and teens are said to be the most challenging times of your parenting journey. I hoped to escape the teens and the terrible twos, but I knew I would feel the stress of these parenting challenges—one child at each end of the growth and behaviour spectrum.

The school year for Kerry would end with a School Leavers' Dinner. It was the highlight of the year for the leavers and the staff. The students had to wear something innovative, and the dinner was held in the school hall. The teachers put together a video presentation of pictures from the school year and highlighted every pupil in some way. After dinner, there was music and some dancing. It almost seemed like an age of innocence for these pupils. They danced in groups together. The boys were awkward, and the girls more sophisticated.

One of the teachers showed the children how to line dance. That helped to get everyone on the dance floor as they stepped to the tune of 'Achy Breaky Heart'. And how did I know all of this? Well, I volunteered to help behind the scenes with the meal and was able to peep through the tuck shop window. Mums were serving some cold drinks and making coffee for the staff. I felt really proud of Kerry. She had those line dance moves all wrapped up and was having a wonderful time. Then I noticed one of her best friends was not on the dance floor. Where was Leslie, I wondered. I knew she had come to the leavers' dinner. Then I saw a little group of boys and girls in the car park. They were hanging out around a minibus. When Leslie saw they were being watched, the door of the bus slammed, and she and another girl from Kerry's class walked back towards the hall. They looked a little unsteady on their feet.

The girls came to the tuck shop window to buy peppermints. I was so shocked and saddened to sense the reason for the mints was to cover up the fact that they had been drinking. Shock and horror set in at the age of these girls and what had been going on in the car park. I did not want to spoil Kerry's leaving party, but I knew I would have to speak up the very next day.

How sad I was at facing this reality. How would I approach the subject? Distressing as it was, perhaps this was a good thing because I should not be naive and think teenagers are not faced with all kinds of temptations. This was an excellent opportunity to speak to Kerry about drug and alcohol abuse. Although it just seemed too soon for such a grown-up conversation, I knew it was something we needed to talk about before becoming the proverbial 'elephant in the living room'. Look at how drinking had affected my own family life. *No*, I said to myself, *I must be strong and courageous*. How do you talk to your teens about drug and alcohol abuse?

The school must have had some indication that there was a problem because a newsletter arrived from the headmaster the next day. One of the topics addressed was 'How to talk to your child about drug and alcohol abuse.' Added to that was an invitation to listen to a talk given by a counsellor from social welfare and a member of the AA. The subject matter for the discussion was about the use of drugs and alcohol among teenagers.

This was a challenging topic, and I was grateful for some guidelines. Peer pressure is one of the most difficult obstacles in a teenager's life. Peer pressure can prompt undesirable behaviour, and for this reason, parents need to have a good relationship with their teenagers.

How to talk to your teenager about alcohol, smoking, and drugs

• Foster an open relationship with your teenager that encourages them to want to talk to you. Try to be a good listener and not too judgemental. Encourage them to be looking for answers to the questions they may be asking already with their friends or in their school circle of fellow students. Try to be there to answer these questions.

• Ask questions, listen to their stories, and make them feel their point of view is valuable. They may have picked up twisted versions of the truth, and you could unravel that.

• If your child has tried out some form of substance and has been a user, try to determine why they chose to experiment with drugs or alcohol. There could be a root cause that you, as a parent, can change.

• Know what to do if you find your child has experimented with drugs or alcohol. Look for signs and symptoms and be knowledgeable yourself as to what substance your child could be using.

• Have your boundaries in place. Be honest with your children about your views and the effects of drugs and alcohol on young minds. Explain some of the risks and the dangerous situations young teens find themselves in due to alcohol and drugs.

• Let your children know you are always there as support, and they can call you any time if they find themselves in danger. Have a code word between you if you feel the need for a rescue word. This word is an alert system if your teen needs to get home urgently.

• Parents should be good role models for their teens. Parents need to be aware of the other influencers in their child's life too. Schedule the talk about drugs and alcohol regardless of whether you suspect your child has been involved with substance abusers or not.

• Consider any family history of drug or alcohol abuse.

The last point resonated rather harshly with me as I remembered the hard days as a child realising my father had a problem, and my mother had to juggle two jobs to make the extra money to raise her family. It prompted me more than ever to talk to Kerry. The weekend after the dance was the ideal opportunity.

At first, Kerry was defensive because I led the conversation towards what I had seen in the car park. She shook her head and denied there was any problem. Then she looked tearful and opened up about her friend Leslie. She said her friend had not been doing well in her exams, and she had started to go to parties with the wrong crowd. I listened to Kerry's concern for her friend, and I was grateful we had opened the door to talking about drinking and using drugs. I offered empathy for Leslie, but at the same time, it was good to caution Kerry and let her know her parents were there to support her.

High school was just around the corner. It was going to be a big step for my daughter. She had been such a great role model as a child growing up, and now, we were facing the teen years. What would we need to do to adjust to these years from childhood to becoming a young adult? We had survived baby days, toddler tantrums, and growing up through primary school. What would make the teen years seem more challenging? There will be growth spurts, physically, emotionally, and cognitively. I hoped it would not be a period of conflict between us, and I wondered what we as a family might have to face.

The library was always a great place to go, not just for the books, but to visit the librarian who was my special friend. I decided to pop round and see Shirley Robson for a coffee date and some input about teenagers. Shirley had two teenage daughters, so she would have some stories to share. I was grateful for Shirley's friendship, and we had kept in contact after I left the school.

Here was a fountain of wisdom in the form of a librarian and teenager mum. I asked Shirl what I should expect from the teen years.

Her input was constructive, and I learned several things that day about the teenager's transformation and what to expect.

One of the first things I learned was that puberty, the physical developmental stage, and adolescence were not the same. Puberty can occur between the ages of 8 and 14, I read, which is quite a wide range of developmental years. Fortunately, Kerry went through this phase in her last year at primary school. The teachers were terrific, with special education sessions about what the girls and boys were going through. We were able to speak as a mother and daughter at this time, which brought us closer. We went on a special mum and daughter outing, and it was a lovely bonding time.

The adolescence phase seems to bring about the change in the behaviour many parents' dread. That was where I wanted some input from Shirley and to find out how she had handled her daughter's teen years. She smiled and said there were different things to look forward to: some good and some not so good. I was probably not going to like all of them.

It's a big-time of transformation for children as they change physically and adjust mentally, she said, and this is what you can look forward to:

• To feeling delighted, frustration, surprise, super excitement, and irritation all thrown into one day with a teen around.

• To *loving* a teenager when you do not really *like* them.

• To needing lots of patience.

• To teenage emotions waiting to explode for any reason.

• To their friends being very important. Teenagers need to be needed by their friends.

• To run around quite a lot, you may feel somewhat like a taxi at times.

• To find it hard to let go sometimes, but accept that it is part of growing up.

Shirley made a great deal of sense. Then in true librarian style, she shared a quote from Walt Disney, the man who brought so much magic into children's lives:

'We keep moving forward, opening new doors, and doing new things because we're curious, and curiosity keeps leading us down new paths.'

New paths for Kerry—going to high school and becoming a teenager—and new paths for me as a parent. I had already noticed Kerry wanted to spend more time in her room. She was becoming more independent and had more homework, and needed study time. We had an extra room outside. It was attached to the workshop and the garage. Kerry asked if she could have this room and paint it up as a teen room for herself. She said she could study better because it was away from the house's noise and her younger siblings. I could see she was keen to have some privacy and space to herself. It was agreed, and she decorated her new room. There was a loo and shower out there too. This gave her the freedom to have her own room and bathroom.

I read this was quite normal as teenagers started to separate from their parents and gain their independence. We did want to make sure she still stayed connected to the family, and one of the rules was she had to pop in and say hello when she got back from school each day. We had a lift club going, which meant I did not have to fetch Kerry every day. This was a great help because I had Nikki and PJ to consider too.

We could see Kerry was trying to find her own identity. Her impatience with her younger siblings were becoming apparent, and it seemed as if her friends were the only important factors in her life. Outings with friends, endless conversations on the phone and loud music seemed to be the norm in Kerry's world. We were grateful that she was still committed to her schoolwork, and all her reports and school assignments were positive. Until a week into the second term!

I noticed Kerry had come home rather late one afternoon. She popped her head around the kitchen door to say hi and went off to her room. On her way, she said she was not hungry and still had her school lunch, so she would skip supper and finish her homework. The following day, she left early. All dressed in her school uniform, hat on her head, and a bag slung over her shoulder. She caught her lift club to school, and I did not think anything further. I dropped Nikki at school, and PJ was going to his playgroup. I did some shopping and halfway round the supermarket the high school called to say, would I please come and collect my daughter, she was waiting in the office.

My heart sank. What was the problem?

I rushed to the school to find Kerry sitting outside the office. She had her hat firmly on her head and a note from the headmistress.

> *'Mrs Lovemore, will you please take Kerry home until further notice,'* said the secretary.

I could see Kerry was terribly upset, and I left the school to get her home and decide what to do from there. When we got in the car, Kerry started to cry and apologise.

I wanted to get home and read the letter. We drove home and went inside and sat down. Kerry still had her hat on.

> *'Now, what is all this about?'* I asked as I started to open the letter.

> *'And for goodness sake, take your hat off!'* I added, not wanting to sound too irritated.

Slowly Kerry removed her hat, and then I realised why she was in trouble. Her hair had been cut into the shortest punk hairstyle I had ever seen. I gasped in shock. My daughter's pretty little bob and neat fringe were as spikey and as spunky as could be. A few long hairs fell on her forehead, and a few others could be seen on her neck. No wonder she had not been joining us for supper in the evening!

Then I read the note from school.

> Dear Mr and Mrs Lovemore,

> The school does not condone outlandish hairstyles. We have sent Kerry home to acknowledge that this is not acceptable, and she may only return to school when her hair looks respectable.

> Please discuss this with Kerry. She is very remorseful, and we are sure this will not happen again.

Both the class teacher and the headmistress had signed the letter.

I could see Kerry was deeply sorry for the punkish hairdo, and she explained that her friends dared her to do something dramatic. We had a good discussion about peer pressure there and then. I realised peer pressure at this age is probably the biggest influence on a teenager's life. There are two forms of peer pressure to consider. One is spoken peer pressure with teens being influenced and dared by other teens to join in activities they know to be bad for them. Actions that would not meet their parent's approval. Then there are the nonverbal pressures of dress code, music, coveting material things that can lead to shoplifting, and pressure to join gangs or undesirable groups. All these activities fall under the umbrella of peer pressure.

Kerry stayed home for two days while we worked out ways to tame her hair. Hair spray and all types of gel were tried out until she looked a bit more respectable. I went to see the headmistress to get more insight into this incident. It was a good interview and helped me understand why Kerry was made an example at that time. The girls in her group and others in the school all learnt some of the dangers of bowing to peer pressure.

Parenting really is an interesting journey, I thought to myself. We never stop learning as parents, and with the ever-increasing world of technology pushing its way into every home, school and even our social lives, it was clear that today's parents are faced with more challenges than the parents of the past. Growing up in a small town, we were excited about drive-in movies, and home computers were extraordinary. Nowadays, there is a far broader spectrum of technology, from iPads to laptops and mobile phones. Large televisions with surround sound and home movie theatres with access to all the latest series and movies are the norms in some homes. Kids of today have exposure to much more technology. It is hard to keep up with the different gadgets available and even monitor the ones you bring into your home.

CHAPTER NINE

RAISING YOUR KIDS IN A WORLD OF TECHNOLOGY

A lbert Einstein, one of the greatest minds we know of, had this to say about technology:

> *'It has become appallingly obvious that our technology has exceeded our humanity.'*

What did he mean by this, and would I find myself agreeing?

Technology has advanced so much, and at the same time, it has become available to younger children as the games and phone apps are incredible. Parents need to be aware that addiction to technology is a consideration for children growing up today. Everything in moderation is the keyword here. Elements of technology are a great advantage for our children. Technology opens doors to many different avenues of study and learning. It is, however, the responsibility of parents to monitor how children use various forms of technology.

I looked at my three children and was struck by their different attitudes to technology. Kerry had been given a mobile phone for her birthday. It was seen to be a necessity for communication as she was in high school now. Kerry enjoyed chats with her friends, but we monitored her phone time. She was busy adjusting to high school, and communication with the school and friends was crucial. Homework apps and communication about sporting events were helpful features.

Nikki did not show any interest in a mobile phone, which solved that problem for the moment. Both the girls were having computer skills lessons at school as we were all aware of the need for understanding technology. I was amazed at how confidently they all managed to change channels on the television. Switch on the microwave and Google information when they need to. I had a laptop for my writing and to help Kerry with her homework when necessary.

It was PJ's reaction to the phone that astonished me. He was at the grab and gobble stage, where everything went in his mouth. My phone was what he wanted desperately! His little hands would reach out to grab the phone. It was as a matter of supreme urgency. It seemed as if he had a potential addiction to technology. When he discovered the buttons, he was not so interested in eating the phone. I bought him the miniature toy version, but he tossed it aside with complete disgust. He wanted the real thing! I knew my husband, and I did not want our son growing up addicted to technology. John was an outdoor kind of guy who loved sport, camping, and fishing. We would have to look for any signs of addiction to technology and be ready to divert or engage our children in other activities. I wondered what the signs of addiction to technology were.

It is a relatively new topic, and this is what I found out:

It is classified as a behavioural addiction. Behavioural addiction is the inability to control or regulate your behaviour towards your interest's device or object. It is an obsessive-compulsive disorder. It becomes an addiction when technology interferes with school, work, social, and family life. The creators of video games and media products are tapping into what is known as a 'compulsion loop'.

Then there is the neurological level of technological addiction. Similar chemicals are released to those experienced through other habits. It is a release of dopamine that sets off the feel-good experience. Your feel-good mood is triggered if you win a game or get more likes on social media. The adolescent brain is still developing, and in particular, the teen phase is one that should be engaging in and learning social behaviour skills. Too much technology affects the brain's wiring and neural pathways —the kind of expectations linked to technology wire the brain strongly for these compulsive loops. Adolescents are building their identity. It is not helpful for character development and emotional growth when the growing teenager's interaction is with a computer game.

Here are some signs to look for if you think your child is becoming addicted to technology.

- A lack of interest in other activities that are not part of the techno devices.
- Irritability or anger when asked to disconnect.
- Continued use of devices even when they should be discontinued.
- Loss of interest in personal hygiene.

• Disinterest in school or college work, preferring the device and games.

Technology has a broad base of applications, and all are related to solving problems in our computer-generated world. One of the most extensive realms of technology is Information Technology, or IT. Computers, mobile phones, iPads, video games, and all kinds of media and electronic gadgets fill IT's realm. There is no end to the amount of electronic and digital products. Children can soon fall prey to the immediate gratification and entrapment found through technology. In the right hands, and with guidance, different forms of technology help children to learn. Whatever our opinion, technology is part of our world and the world our children will grow up in.

Technology can be divided into the good and the bad. I looked at both sides to weigh the effects of technology and the different devices found in most homes today.

Starting with television. Almost every home has a television these days, and some homes have more than one because different family members want to watch their own programmes. Most children learn from an early age how to switch on the TV and change channels too. The plus side of television is the early learning skills it can teach. Excellent wildlife programmes enhance general knowledge. However, parents must be selective and not use the television as a glorified babysitter. Watching hours of 'Looney Tunes' is not going to enhance your child's vocabulary.

Selecting the right programmes encourages literacy and helps with numeracy and early learning skills. However, it is wise to observe your child while watching these shows. Are they just sitting in front of the TV in a trance? Or are they engaged with the characters and interacting with the story?

Watching too much TV makes children anti-social, and their desire to run and play with physical interaction is lessened. Violent TV programmes have a negative effect on children. Television robs children of their willingness to run and play. Many children are eating their suppers in front of the TV and not engaging in social behaviour.

Other electronic devices, like computers and smartphones, should be monitored by parents. As children get older, their fascination with these devices increases, and they have access to more media.

I found these guidelines immensely helpful because the media is not something we can escape. What should parents do about monitoring the media?

• Decide on the benefits you see in a particular programme and then try to watch them together. In that way, you can add to the experience.

• Try not to use the TV as a babysitter.

• Limit television and electronic devices because they take away the benefits of moving and playing.

• Include imaginative games in your child's time at home. They are an essential part of being prepared for preschool.

• Watch out for instant gratification promoted by electronic devices. It is not conducive to sharing and taking turns. It does not promote good social behaviour.

• Interaction with toys and physically enjoying the outdoors is essential. Electronic devices cannot replace good old fashioned play experiences.

I was just letting these points sink in when I heard the most peculiar noise coming from the front garden. A high-pitched screech, followed by splashing and laughter, echoed across the lawn. I was not sure what I would find. It sounded like someone could be in pain, but the laughter made it sound like someone was having fun.

I opened the front door, and the sight I saw made me join in the laughter too. Nikki had filled the wheelbarrow with water and had added some of PJ's bath toys to the mix. She was pushing him around the garden while the water sloshed out of the wheelbarrow. PJ was clinging on for all he was worth with his big, brown eyes wide open. The screech was the front wheel of the rusty wheelbarrow, and the shrieks of laughter came from Nikki and PJ. I was about to explode when I realised they were having a good time. Nikki stopped in her tracks when she saw me, and I could tell she was very unsure how to react.

> *'What are you doing?'* I asked as the wheelbarrow came to a halt.

All the water sloshed out onto the grass while the baby hung on to the sides with a massive grin on his face.

> *'I made a pool for PJ. It's a porta-pool,'* said Nikki with such a cheeky look on her face.

Well, I couldn't help laughing out loud. That is when I knew my two little ones would not fall prey to the techno demon. Here they were ticking all the boxes for imaginative play far away from any of the media.

- Creative—tick
- Sociable—tick
- Outdoors—tick

.

- Physical—tick

I couldn't resist taking pictures on my smartphone, and I knew I would be rushing off to post them to my Facebook page! I realised we are all part of technology, but the degree to which it dominates our lives is what we all need to be wary of.

The most significant influence technology has had on family life is how it has influenced children's play activities. Children learn through play, and their bodies benefit from physical exercise outdoors as much as possible. Our children are lucky to be growing up in a country that values outdoor physical playtimes. Children are encouraged to be outside and interact with other children. In many families, technology has changed this aspect of play for children.

I found myself wondering about the dangers of not playing outside enough.

- Top of the list came insufficient exercise, leading to obesity. Parents and schools are making a great effort to change this and are aware of the dangers of a lack of exercise.
- There are other benefits to spending time outdoors, and these are the positive effects on the body of fresh air and sunlight, giving the body vitamin D to boost the immune system.
- Children who play outside sleep better and are less exposed to harmful blue light from computer and phone screens.
- Technology changes the way children socialise, and high amounts of screen time and social media levels can influence the way children feel about themselves.

These were just a few of the points relating to outdoor play and social behaviour. I had a feeling there was much more to know about technology and its influences, good and bad, on family life.

I found myself looking for information on technology. There were so many questions to answer.

How does technology affect family life?

What can technology do to children's minds and thinking?

How could I find out about the good and the bad influences of technology?

There were some excellent books and inspiring quotes. I wrote them in my journal to see how I could learn from them and if there was wisdom out there in cyberspace to use in our everyday life. The life of a family. A father, mother, and three children at different stages of their childhood. I realised I was the fortunate mum of a teen, a pre-teen, and a toddler—what a beautiful cross-section of developmental phases.

Creative personalities like Pablo Picasso
had very little to say about technology.

*'Computers are useless. They can only
give you answers.'*

*Well, that was something to think
about.*

*Then Andy Crouch, author of a book
called The Tech-Wise Family, said:*

*'Find the room where your family
spends the most time and ruthlessly
eliminate the things that ask little of
you and develop little in you.'*

Where was I going with all this information?

Suddenly there was a loud yell from the lounge, and I heard
Kerry's favourite music blasting forth from the television. What
on earth was going on? I was sure the neighbours would be
calling any moment to ask me to turn down the music. I rushed
through to see what all the noise was about. I was about to burst
into laughter as I saw not Kerry but my husband jumping up and
down in front of the TV. He appeared to be doing some kind of
ritual dance while a series of boy band singers shouted out loud
on *Pop Shop*!

Then I realised that John was not dancing to the beat of the music. He was having a complete meltdown and was furious.

> *'Someone has taped over my latest David Attenborough documentaries I wanted to watch this weekend,'* he yelled and scowled at me.

Oh boy, this was big trouble. John loved his wildlife documentaries, and David Attenborough's were his all-time favourites.

The girls were called into the lounge to explain. They were sorry. It seemed that by mistake, Kerry had taped her episode of music over her dad's documentary. Technology had transformed John into a furious parent and the teenager into a disappointing music fan. There was no winner here because John lost out on David Attenborough, and Kerry's music was immediately erased. She apologised to her dad, and I promised to outsource the documentaries for John. This was the catalyst that made me research the effects of technology on family life. I needed answers to the many questions buzzing around in my head.

The list was long, but I started with the first question:

1. What qualifies as technology?

Technology is an extensive base of methods and processes that affect every aspect of our world today. Out of all the technological descriptions, IT, information technology, and technology for children are probably the most pertinent to parents and home devices. Technology for children can start in early childhood with the development of eye-hand coordination and fine motor skills—online games and computer games, and other devices considered to be educational.

There is a wide variety of devices available to children and programmes helping with reading skills, maths, general knowledge, and more. The common denominator I found was most of these devices use screens to send out the information or provide the games. Screen time is what has invaded our homes and children's line of vision. Smartphones, tablets, iPads, and many apps to download games, music, and videos are all available to entertain and educate. One piece of advice I found appropriate was to choose something you can enjoy sharing with your child. Especially at a young age, shared time on the device makes the technological experience more meaningful. It gives you, the parent, an indication of the value of the programme.

That led to my next question.

2. How much screen time is recommended?

I know from my developmental psychology training that unstructured playtime is more beneficial to young, growing children. Children under the age of two learn more from doing and being physically interactive with adults or other children. The early years' introduction to screen time should be to watch interactive programmes promoting music and movement and listening to stories. Preferably with a parent to interact with their child. I found out that the American Academy of Paediatrics discourages media use for children younger than 18 to 24 months. Children between the ages of 2 and 5 years were recommended to use one hour of screen time per day. Older children were not given specific limits, but there needed to be limited media time to suit every family's boundaries. This research came to light on the Mayo Clinic website. Here are some interesting points I picked up.

• The quality of media time is essential, and parents are advised to preview programmes and apps before releasing them to their children.

• Parents are advised to look for interactive options that engage children and encourage them to participate in some way.

• Parents should use parental controls to block or filter access to different internet programmes.

• Discuss different programmes with your child, so you are familiar with what they are watching.

• Avoid advertisements where possible as children find it difficult, to tell the truth from exaggeration and sensationalism.

• Avoid fast-paced programmes your child will have difficulty keeping up with. This often leads to mindless viewing and no interaction.

• Encourage critical thinking and evaluate different programmes with your child.

Tips for older children were more about monitoring times and quality control.

• Media time should not occur during homework time unless it is part of project research or confirming a school-related event.

• Keep devices and charging of devices out of the bedroom and stop screen time at least an hour before going to sleep.

• Set out and enforce screen time limits and encourage some unplugged and unstructured playtime or outdoor activity.

• Create times when there are no techno devices allowed. Even create tech-free zones in the house like the dining room.

• Limit your own use of technology as an example to your children.

I discovered something else along the way, and that led to another point.

3. What essential things should we teach our children so that they behave appropriately while using technology?

• Explaining to children the adverse effects of cyberbullying, sexting, and sharing personal information online.

• Teach your child not to share anything online that they would not like the whole world to see forever!

• Monitor your child's online and media connections for safety and security.

• Encourage sensible use of media and have realistic boundaries that encourage safe and sensible use of technical devices.

These were more of the physical and technical questions I had, but what about the mental issues. What are some of the effects of screen time on the developing brains of our children? Were there good and bad aspects to consider? Yes, we can see the physical and the social impact, but how do parents measure the mental side of technology.

4. What are the mental effects of screen time on children?

• The brain chemical dopamine is released while children are exposed to screen time. This is like a 'digital drug', and children can have difficulty withdrawing from excessive use of digital devices.

• Children's eyes are attracted to the bright light and the colours on electronic devices. The blue light from the screen can affect the brain's internal clock and suppress standard sleep signals. A delay in melatonin release can result in insomnia and make it more difficult for children to fall asleep.

• Clinical research has indicated a correlation between excessive screen time and frontal lobe development, impacting impulse control, personality, reasoning, and empathy.

• A comparison between brain activity during screen time and reading time showed clearly that reading increases brain activity.

• Smartphones in the bedroom were linked to depression. The blue light elevates cortisol, the fight or flight stress hormone. Experts recommend a night setting for these devices to reduce the hours of exposure to blue light.

• Definite changes in brain chemistry have been noted by the Radiological Society of North America who found evidence of changes in the brain's reward system from children addicted to technology. Addicted participants had higher scores relating to depression, insomnia, anxiety, and impulsivity.

These were all very thought-provoking comments, but there must be some good in all these devices. After reading the effects of technology on the brain, my next question was to find the good things these devices bring.

5. What are the advantages of technology for our children?

• Visually, the following something on a screen and participating by using their hands to engage with the object improves eye-hand coordination.

• Helps children develop language skills by engaging with stories and picture word cards and the different language development programmes. With parental guidance, these programmes' value needs to be assessed to be sure they are interactive.

• Developmentally appropriate programmes can increase readiness to learn reading and maths skills, problem-solving and thinking skills. Once again, parents should ensure these programmes are interactive.

• Some games and applications help children to pay more attention to detail; they increase visual awareness.

• Games and on-screen rewards motivate children to complete tasks. They want to keep trying and overcome challenges.

• Problem-solving skills are encouraged through puzzles and games. Different programmes offer visual problem-solving opportunities.

• Technology exposes children to broader horizons and things they would not see every day. They can explore different countries and learn about our natural world through beautiful wildlife programmes geared to different ages.

Yes, these answers helped provide a better idea of technology's effects—the advantages and disadvantages. I had one last question in my mind. It was about overcoming bad habits if your child has become addicted to technology. This must be a very real and rather worrying thing for parents who may not have grown up with a technology background.

I know John, for example, had some struggles with mastering his mobile phone after growing up on a farm. Kerry had helped him on some occasions, and that was an endearing thing to see. Her dad insisted on referring to 'WhatsApp' as 'what's up', and he was proud of his use of current slang for something on the phone. I could safely say my husband was not addicted to technology. What would help the parents of children who were suffering from this addiction?

This was a thought-provoking quote from Nassim Nicholas Taleb, an essayist, mathematical statistician, and risk analyst.

He wrote: 'The difference between technology and slavery is that slaves were fully aware that they were not free!'

Wow, that was something to think about. We have to be aware of how technology can entrap our children unknowingly.

6. How to help children who are addicted to technology?

• Look at your own habits. Are you, as a parent, always on a screen device of some sort? Checking your phone and possibly having some issues of your own? Set the example to your children that you want them to see.

• Encourage electronic free playdates. Invite children over to socialise without using electronic devices.

• Turn off notifications on your phone for less interference and evidence of technology. Catch up later.

• Have a timer or device to alert time spent on technology and move on to another activity.

• Set some boundaries, especially if you did not have any before becoming aware your child was becoming addicted to technology.

• Become more aware of what your children are involved in.

- Limit screen time slowly to avoid withdrawal. Then over time, with consistent monitoring and offering alternatives to using technology for recreation, your child will begin to make the necessary changes in their lifestyle. It will take perseverance and commitment.

Alternatives to technology were what John and I discussed the next day. It was Saturday and John thought we should go out for a family picnic and he was going to do some fishing.

> *'I think we should all go fishing,'* said John.

> 'Phishing, no Dad, that is bad. We learnt about phishing in IT yesterday,' said Kerry with a horrified look on her face.

> *'No,'* said John. *'Fishing is very relaxing. We can all sit outside and enjoy being in the country.'*

I realised that Kerry was referring to phishing in technology terms. It is not good, it's like cyber theft, and she was right to be horrified. Fishing had to mean the outdoor sport kind, not the computer variety. Getting out as a family was important because phishing and fishing should never be confused in our children's minds.

It was too complicated to explain, but I encouraged a balance of activities to make sure our family values still included good old-fashioned picnics and fishing trips. Getting out and about was important.

On the way back from the fishing spot, Nikki entertained us with one of her knock-knock jokes.

'Knock knock?' said Nikki.

'Who's there?' we all responded.

'Fish,' Nikki said.

'Fish who?' asked Kerry.

'Fish who?' repeated PJ.

Nikki paused long enough for the words to sink in, then she replied.

> *'Bless you, Kerry and PJ!'*

Everyone laughed at the silly joke. And I thought how blessed I was.

I had three lovely children to be grateful for and a husband who supported our family values.

REVIEW

Customer Reviews

Share your thoughts with other customers

Write a customer review

I would be incredibly thankful if you could just take 60 seconds to write a brief review on Amazon, even if it's just a few sentences.

https://www.amazon.com/review/create-review/asin=B09PZYVJR2

Conclusion

Magic moments come every so often when, as a mother, one can sit and reflect on memories and parenting joys. A family day out was always one of them. It was uplifting to look back on pictures and see notes in my journals, recording many of my experiences.

'Is parenting just a joy ride?' I ask myself. I am shocked by my answer, as I say...

'No, not a joy ride, but a roller coaster ride.'

I am struck by the analogy of a roller coaster ride and my parenting journey. There are moments of joy as you slowly climb to the peak of the roller coaster and look out on a beautiful view. Then there are the profound stomach-churning moments as the roller coaster plummets to the depths of the ride. I am not a thrill and spills person. I feel dizzy just watching a roller coaster. Going to funfairs is not my idea of a great way to spend an afternoon.

Comparing parenting to a roller coaster ride brings home the reality of the times we face as parents. Imagine being on 'Millennium Force' or 'Ring Racer', some of the world's fastest roller coaster rides. 'Steel Vengeance', 'Fury', and 'The Revenge of the Mummy' resonated well with some of our more challenging parenting experiences.

Parenting, I had to admit to myself, is not all about scary twists and turns. Our three children do not always send us into the fastest and steepest parenting rides of all time. There are gentle walks around the garden or the park, enjoying the outdoors and the wonders of nature through a child's eyes. There are the thrills of seeing a child conquer difficulties or shine at school for some academic or sporting competition. Added to these moments is the joy of watching a father teach his son to fish with an ever-eager daughter in the mix. Teaching and learning family values can never be overestimated.

The children are in bed, and I have this moment to reflect. I looked across the room at my husband, and I sighed with relief. He looked at me and raised his eyebrows as he expected something dramatic to come forth from my side of the room.

>*'What's the matter?' he asked. 'Sharing is caring.'* A
>parenting phrase he had learned.

I had to confess there was nothing the matter right at that moment. I was just feeling really content. It was my 'Desiderata' reminder.

'Go placidly amid the noise and haste,
and remember what peace there may
be in silence. As far as possible, without
surrender, be on good terms with all
persons.'

It is one of those moments when there is some peace in the silence in our home.

The children were in bed, and in the quiet of the evening, I reflected on this book I had just completed. This was my first book, and I felt a surge of pride in the content. Not just any parenting book, but one that took pieces of my own life and mixed them with parenting advice. True stories and the truth to be told. I had read parts out to my husband and watched him smile at the funny stories and look concerned at some more serious anecdotes. Sadly, he shook his head at the truth behind the teen lecture from the school on drugs and alcohol.

'We need to be there to help young people through the difficulties they face in our modern world,' he said.

He nodded encouragingly at my take on technology. We both agreed technology was here to stay, but it had to be monitored and carefully controlled while children were still vulnerable.

I am grateful for John's encouragement to put together this original and personal approach to parenting guidebooks. I wanted to share from my own experiences, and at the same time, impart knowledge and practical advice along the way. I hoped parents would relate to the chapters on basic parenting styles while seeing the world through a child's eye. Communication is always a vital topic for parenting guidance. Setting boundaries and discipline seems to be a subject most parents want to know more about.

The challenges of school life take up a good part of the parenting journey. Children go through several phases of education while they grow up and develop into young adults. I was so grateful to use my counselling skills and interact with parents and teachers at the school. Dealing with aggressive behaviour, peer pressure, and academic difficulties are part and parcel of school life. My own family is not a model suburban family. Having problems with my own gave me more empathy for the difficulties of others.

This concludes my first parenting book. Sharing my life and the thrills of family life along the way with parenting advice. I have tried to cover the most current topics parents seem to have on their minds. The chapters that include advice on addictions, especially alcohol and drug abuse, were challenging to include. Substance abuse is a real struggle for many of our teenage children. Technology, too, has its advantages and disadvantages. Finding a balance in the electronic world is so important.

I found juggling three children's schedules at different development stages an exciting but sometimes exhausting, balancing act. Each child, at each age, has been different. Two girls did not fit the same mould as each other. Then we added a boy to the family dynamic. Yes, raising a boy was different. How did we all keep our sanity?

Parents of the teen set had a mums and teens group going on their phones. Encouraging notes and keeping track of our teens seemed to help us feel connected. Then Nikki's age group, still at the pre-teen phase, just kept the mums of that group very busy with all the activities they were exploring. Social butterflies that they were. PJ, now an active toddler, added a fascinating new dimension to our family. I joined a mum and toddler group to make sure PJ had time to interact with his peers. Toddler talks were fun to host, but my love of writing was the catalyst for this book. It has been very gratifying to write each chapter. I am already thinking of other topics as there is so much to investigate in the parenting field.

> *'I think you should start a blog,'* said John. *'Share your parenting ideas and get more enjoyment out of your writing.'*

> *Could this be the start of something new?* I asked myself.

Not a roller coaster ride, but one of those hop-on and hop-off bus tours. The kind you rode on if you went to visit London. Writing for parents and still being involved with my family sounded like a perfect new beginning.

Just as Winston Churchill said:

> *'Now, this is not the end. It is not even the beginning of the end.*

> *But it is, perhaps, the end of the beginning.'*

The possibility of sharing parenting ideas and knowing this is not the end but a new beginning is a fascinating prospect.

I would like to take the time to THANK YOU for purchasing this book. As an author, it means a lot to me! For this reason, I would like to send you a copy of **'The Ultimate Parenting Guide'** as an appreciation and gratitude. Click the link below for your **FREE COPY!**

THE ULTIMATE PARENTING GUIDE

For Parents with paperback & Hardcover

www.lovemoreservices.com

ABOUT AUTHOR

Christina Lovemore lives in Sydney, Australia, with her husband John and their three children. Kerry, Nikki and Peter John, affectionately known as P.J.

Christina was born in the South of England, near Portsmouth. Her parents decided to travel. Settling down to life in different places was
challenging. Christina's parents went through tough times, ending in a permanent separation. It was during these times Christina found herself looking after her younger brothers. She had to learn about parenting the hard way. She found solace through journaling and writing short stories.

Christina became interested in child care and decided to study teaching. She gained qualifications in both primary and pre-primary education. Christina found developmental psychology of particular interest. She went on to further her tertiary education through the study of family counselling. Christina was involved in school counselling and hosted successful parenting workshops.

It was during the early days of her teaching career she met her husband, John. After the birth of their first child, Kerry, they decided to move to Australia to connect with John's family. When her second daughter, Nikki, arrived, Christina became involved in school life again. Teaching and parenting went hand in hand very well.

Christina felt at ease in the library. Books, children and counselling parents made the perfect package, all her favourite things rolled into one. But life has a habit of dishing out some things differently!

The arrival of a third child prompted Christina to become a stay at home mum. However, she still wanted to share her knowledge and experience of parenting. She decided to write a book. A parenting book that embraced her love of storytelling with her desire to impart practical parenting knowledge.

This was the beginning of <u>Learn More and Lovemore</u> books. And many more writing opportunities for Christina.

Glossary

Themes in the book you can look back on for more understanding of the topic.

Themes to review for tips and information

.

REFERENCE

Barre Dr. Robin. (4th July 2018.) www.heysigmund.com Parenting from a Love/Fear Spectrum. Pub. Excite Media.

Bell Marlesha (25th June 2020) www.proquest.com Changing the Culture of Consent: Teaching Young Children Personal Boundaries. Pub. Proquest Publishing.

Cherry Kendra, (4th April 2020.) www.verywellmind.com Why Parenting Styles Matter when Raising Children. Pub. Dotdash Publishing.

Content and Development Team. (31st August 2020) www.raisingchildren.net.au Communicating well with Babies and Toddlers. Pub. Raising Children Network (Australia)

Erikson Erik (26th June 2020) www.verywellmind.com Stages of psychological development. Pub. Dotdash Publishing

Fader Sarah (16th April 2020) www.suportiv.com Parenting: How to set Boundaries with Kids. Pub. Supportive Publishers.

Grose Jessica. (13th January 2021) wwwnytimes.com The Psychology Behind Sibling Rivalry. Pub. New York Times Company.

Kneteman   Lindsay.   (24th   September   2020) www.todaysparent.com How to talk to your kids about sex. Pub: St Joseph Communications.

Kumon. Blog (Nov. 2016) www.kumon.co.uk The Importance of Good Communication Skills. Pub. Kumon Europe and Africa Ltd.

Lee Katherine (1st April 2021) www.verywellfamily.com How to Set Healthy Boundaries for Kids. Pub.Dotdash Publishing.

Lee Katherine (1st May 2020) www.verywellfamily.com Why being an authoritative parent is the best approach. Pub. DotDash Publishing.

Mahon Mary. (23rd Feb. 2021) www.infobloom.com What is Child Psychology? Pub. Conjecture Cooperation.

Morin Amy. LCSW (12th July 2019) www.verywellfamily.com 4 Types of Parenting Styles and their Effect on Kids. Pub.

DotDash Publishers. REFERENCE | 203 Myers Pam (17th Nov. 2014) www.childdevelopmentinfo.com 5 Tips for Parenting Together When your Styles Conflict. Pub. Parenting Today.

Pulianda   Megha   MS   (14th   August   2017) www.psychologytoday.com Love and Fear in Parenting. Sussex Publishers.

Reyzelman Alina (August 2018) www.alinareyzelman.com Different Contexts of Child Psychology: Psycho Social Development. Pub. Alinareyzelman.

Selva Joaquin Bsc (24th February 2021) www.positivepsychology.com How to Set Healthy Boundaries. Pub. Positive Psychology. Staff WWMG. (26th March 2018) www.westernwashington-medicalgroup.com What is Psychology and Why is it Important?/blog/Child Psychology. Pub. Sitecrafting.

Thompson Hilary (7th February 2018) www.motherly.com What is the best parenting style to raise a successful child. Pub. Newswhip.

Vogt Caitlin (20th July 2019) www.mycollegeoptions.com 10 Tips to Starting High School. Pub. My College Options Inc

Printed in Great Britain
by Amazon

82889394R00114